BOONE COUNTY LIBRARY

2040 910 424 829 3

W9-BNX-683

WITHDRAWN

BOONE COUNTY PUBLIC LIBRARY
BURLINGTON, KY 41005
www.bcpl.org

NOV 2 2 2005

WITHDRAWN

The Arab-Israeli Conflict

The Arab-Israeli Conflict

Other books in The Lucent Library of Conflict in the Middle East series include:

Human Rights in the Middle East
The Middle East: An Overview
The Palestinians
U.S. Involvement in the Middle East: Inciting Conflict

THE LUCENT LIBRARY OF CONFLICT IN THE MIDDLE EAST

The Arab-Israeli Conflict

By Debra A. Miller

LUCENT BOOKS

An imprint of Thomson Gale, a part of The Thomson Corporation

Detroit • New York • San Francisco • San Diego • New Haven, Conn. • Waterville, Maine • London • Munich

THOMSON
GALE
™

On cover: A Palestinian youth throws stones at a tank during clashes
with Israeli troops in the West Bank town of Nablus.

Lauri Friedman, Series Editor

© 2005 Thomson Gale, a part of the Thomson Corporation.

Thomson and Star Logo are trademarks and Gale and Lucent Books are registered trademarks used
herein under license.

For more information, contact
Lucent Books
27500 Drake Rd.
Farmington Hills, MI 48331-3535
Or you can visit our Internet site at http://www.gale.com

ALL RIGHTS RESERVED.
No part of this work covered by the copyright hereon may be reproduced or used in any form or by any
means—graphic, electronic, or mechanical, including photocopying, recording, taping, Web
distribution, or information storage retrieval systems—without the written permission of the publisher.

Every effort has been made to trace the owners of copyrighted material.

LIBRARY OF CONGRESS CATALOGING-IN-PUBLICATION DATA

The Arab-Israeli conflict / Debra A. Miller.
   p. cm. — (The Lucent library of conflict in the Middle East)
Summary: Discusses the history of Israel and Palestine, the wars between Arabs and
Israelis, and the conflict that exists today between the two groups.
   Includes bibliographical references and index.
   ISBN 1-59018-491-2
   1. Arab-Israeli conflict—Juvenile literature. I. Miller, Debra A. II. Title. III. Series: Lucent
library of conflict in the Middle East.
   DS119.7.A67185 2004
   956.04—dc22
                                                                      2004006169

Printed in the United States of America

CONTENTS

FOREWORD

On May 29, 2004, a group of Islamic terrorists attacked a housing compound in Khobar, Saudi Arabia, where hundreds of petroleum industry employees, many of them Westerners, lived. The terrorists ran through the complex, taking hostages and murdering people they considered infidels. At one point, they came across an Iraqi-American engineer who was Muslim. As the helpless stranger stood frozen before them, the terrorists debated whether or not he deserved to die. "He's an American, we should shoot him," said one of the terrorists. "We don't shoot Muslims," responded another. The militants calmly discussed the predicament for several minutes and finally came to an agreement. "We are not going to shoot you," they told the terrorized man. After preaching to him about the righteousness of Islam, they continued their bloody spree.

The engineer's life was spared because the terrorists decided that his identity as a Muslim overrode all other factors that marked him as their enemy. Among the unfortunate twenty-two others killed that day were Swedes, Americans, Indians, and Filipinos whose identity as foreigners or Westerners or, as the terrorists proclaimed, "Zionists and crusaders," determined their fate. Although the Muslim engineer whose life was spared had far more in common with his murdered coworkers than with the terrorists, in the militants' eyes he was on their side.

The terrorist attacks in Khobar typify the conflict in the Middle East today, where fighting is often done along factionalist lines. Indeed, historically the peoples of the Middle East have been unified not by national identity but by intense loyalty to a tribe, ethnic group, and above all, religious sect. For example, Iraq is home to Sunni Muslims, Shiite Muslims, Kurds, Turkomans, and Christian Assyrians who identify themselves by ethnic and religious affiliation first, and as Iraqis second. When conflict erupts, ancient, sometimes obscure alliances determine whom they fight with and whom they fight against. Navigating this complex labyrinth of loyalties is key to understanding conflict in the Middle East, because these identities generate not only passionate allegiance to one's own group but also fanatic intolerance and fierce hatred of others.

Russian author Anton Chekhov once astutely noted, "Love, friendship, respect do not unite people as much as a common hatred for something." His words serve as a slogan for conflict in the Middle East, where religious belief and tribal allegiances perpetuate strong codes of honor and revenge, and hate is used to motivate people to join in a common cause. The methods of generating hatred in the Middle East are pervasive and overt. After Friday noon prayers, for example, imams in both Sunni and Shiite mosques deliver fiery sermons that inflame tensions between the sects that run high in nearly every Muslim country where the two groups coexist. With similar intent to incite hatred, Iranian satellite television programs broadcast forceful messages to Shiite Muslims across the Middle East, condemning certain groups as threats to Shiite values.

Perhaps some of the most astounding examples of people bonding in hatred are found in the Israeli-Palestinian conflict. In the Palestinian territories, men, women, and children are consistently taught to hate Israel, and even to die in the fight for Palestine. In spring 2004, the terrorist group Hamas went so far as to launch an online children's magazine that demonizes Israel and encourages youths to become suicide bombers. On the other hand, some sectors of Israeli society work hard to stereotype and degrade Palestinians in order to harden Israelis against the Palestinian cause. Is-

raeli journalist Barry Chamish, for example, dehumanizes Palestinians when he writes, "The Palestinians know nothing of the creation of beauty, engage in no serious scholarship, pass nothing of greatness down the ages. Their legacy is purely of destruction."

This type of propaganda inflames tensions in the Middle East, leading to a cycle of violence that has thus far proven impossible to break. Terrorist organizations send suicide bombers into Israeli cities to retaliate for Israeli assassinations of Palestinian leaders. The Israeli military, in response, leads incursions into Palestinian villages to demolish blocks upon blocks of homes, shops, and schools, further impoverishing an already desperate community. To avenge the destruction and death left in the wake of the incursions, Palestinians recruit more suicide bombers to launch themselves at civilian targets in Israeli cities. Neither side is willing to let a violent attack go unreciprocated, undermining nonviolent attempts to mediate the conflict, and the vicious cycle continues.

The books in the Lucent Library of Conflict in the Middle East help readers understand this embattled region of the world. Annotated bibliographies provide readers with ideas for further research, while fully documented primary and secondary source quotations enhance the text. Each book in the series explores a different facet of conflict in the Middle East; together they provide students with a wealth of information as well as launching points for further study and discussion.

INTRODUCTION

The Long Road to Peace

The Arab-Israeli conflict is a dispute over a small area of land historically known as Palestine, sandwiched between Egypt, Jordan, Syria, and Lebanon and next to the Mediterranean Sea. It is a historical place, home to three religions—Judaism, Christianity, and Islam. It is also the site of more than fifty years of violent and bloody fighting between European Jews who settled in the area and native Palestinian Arabs, who with help from neighboring Arab countries, have fought against Jewish presence in their lands. In recent decades, however, the two sides have begun a difficult and wrenching process toward peace, which has brought them close, but not close enough, to a permanent peace agreement.

Today, most of historical Palestine is part of the modern nation of Israel. Jews began settling in Palestine as early as the 1880s, to escape the persecution and discrimination they faced as Jews (called anti-Semitism) in European countries such as France, England, Germany, and Russia. Israel's declaration of independence in 1948, however, sparked a long string of wars between Israel and neighboring Arab nations, who refused to recognize a Jewish state in what had been Arab territory for thirteen centuries. These conflicts not only created hundreds of thousands of Palestinian Arab refugees; they also pushed Israel to develop a strong military and to seize additional lands. For example, during what is called the Six-Day War in 1967, Israel seized various Arab territories beyond its original borders, inhabited by Palestinians. Much of this land, in the West Bank, Gaza, and the Golan Heights, today remains occupied by Israeli troops and largely under Israeli control.

A Cycle of Violence

This seizure of additional territory by Israel, and Israel's policy of moving Israeli settlers into the new territories, became a central issue in a brutal battle between Israelis and Palestinians and led to a cycle of violence that continues to this day. To the Israelis, who have been attacked by neighboring Arab countries repeatedly and who have been the target of countless Palestinian terrorist strikes, settlements and military outposts in Palestinian territories are seen as necessary to defend Israel from the enemies that surround it. They provide a defensive buffer that allows Israel to station troops deep into Palestinian areas to repel Arab invasions or attacks.

For the Palestinians, however, the settlements are seen as a continual assault on Palestinian dignity and freedom of movement and a threat to their hopes for an independent Palestinian nation. The settlements are scattered across the West Bank and Gaza. They divide Palestinian lands, often taking

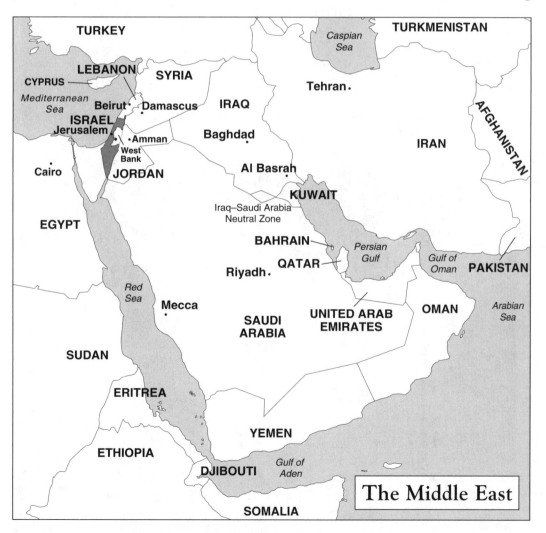

The Middle East

the best areas for Israelis and leaving Palestinians with less desirable areas. Israel sends troops to protect the settlements from frequent Arab attacks, uses up precious resources such as water for Israeli needs, and builds roads connecting the settlements with each other. This network of Israeli activity restricts the Palestinians from freely moving within their own territories, confronts them daily with the presence of Israeli troops at roadblocks and checkpoints, and condemns many Palestinians to unemployment and poverty. As a result, many Palestinians have lost almost all hope for a better future.

In this context, Palestinian militant groups such as the Palestine Liberation Organization (PLO) and Hamas have felt justified in using terrorism to strike at Israeli targets in the hopes that the cost of Israeli lives will convince Israel to remove settlements and leave the occupied territories. Typically, these strikes have not been limited to Israeli military targets, but instead have been consciously directed at innocent Israeli civilians, to shock and terrorize as much as possible. The attacks are carried out by suicide bombers, young Palestinian men and occasionally women who agree to travel into Israel and blow themselves up to become martyrs for the Palestinian cause.

The desperation and hopelessness of Palestinians has also been voiced in two popular uprisings, called intifadas, in

Palestinian boys throw stones at an Israeli tank in the West Bank, an Israeli-controlled Arab territory in the Middle East.

which Palestinians from all walks of life spontaneously protest and riot against Israeli occupation policies, striking out against Israelis with both words and weapons. Israel, in turn, responds to terrorist attacks and intifada rioting with brutal military crackdowns in the occupied territories and strikes at militant leaders, thereby continuing the horrible cycle of violence.

Decades of this tit-for-tat violence in the Middle East have caused many deaths and injuries for both sides, as well as unprecedented devastation to Palestinian property, economy, and society. Indeed, over the years not only countless soldiers and civilians but also peacemakers themselves have paid with their lives. For example, both Egypt's President Anwar Sadat and Israel's Prime Minister Yitzhak Rabin were assassinated by zealots from their own countries who opposed their peace efforts.

An Elusive Peace

In the 1990s, after efforts by Egypt and Jordan to represent the Palestinians failed, Israelis and Palestinians finally sat down together to hold peace talks to try to end the violence. In 1993, for example, talks between Israeli and Palestinian negotiators in Oslo, Norway, produced the historic Oslo Agreements, which provided for Palestinian self-rule in certain portions of the occupied territories. Yasir Arafat, leader of the PLO, was elected as president of a newly created Palestinian government called the Palestinian Authority, and peace talks continued on permanent peace options, such as the creation of an independent Palestinian state and Israeli withdrawal from the territories it won in 1967. These talks ultimately collapsed in 2000, but provided hope that someday the two parties could arrive at a permanent peace.

After still more violence, the latest round of peace negotiations began in 2003 when U.S. president George W. Bush, after consultations with Russia, the European Union, and the United Nations (UN), proposed a new peace plan called the "Road Map." Negotiations, however, quickly stalled amid continuing Palestinian suicide bombings and Israeli retaliation. Peace in the Middle East, therefore, still seems like a distant dream.

CHAPTER 1

Roots of the Conflict

Early in its history the region of Palestine spawned several of the world's religions. Many biblical events of both the Old and New Testament took place there, making it important to both Jews and Christians. Centuries later, when Arab tribes conquered it, Palestine became an Arab region holy to Muslims. Beginning in 1517 the area became part of the Ottoman Empire and for many centuries Muslims, Jews, and Christians all lived in Palestine, with each religious community running its own affairs. This balance of power changed, however, beginning in the late nineteenth century, as Jews began immigrating to the area with the support of Britain and other European powers.

Jewish Immigration to Palestine

Late in the 1880s Jews from Europe began resettling in Palestine as part of a movement called "Zionism," which sought to create a homeland for Jews in Palestine. The Zionist movement began in Europe, where many of the world's Jews had resided after being expelled from Palestine by the Romans in the first century A.D. Historically, Jews in these European countries were discriminated against and treated as outsiders by Europeans. For example, Jews were forced to live in ghettos and were not permitted to own land or hold certain jobs. Conditions improved somewhat in western and central Europe, but as late as 1881 Russia imposed openly anti-Semitic and highly oppressive policies, limiting work opportunities for Jews and even denying them police protection from violent anti-Semitic mobs that killed Jews and looted Jewish neighborhoods. This anti-Semitism led many Jews to desire their own homeland.

A worldwide Zionist organization was first founded by Theodor Herzl, a Jewish correspondent for a Viennese newspaper. In 1896 Herzl wrote a pamphlet called *Der Judenstaat* (*The Jewish State*) in which he argued that Jews were a nation without a land and that the world powers should therefore provide them with a territory where they could create a country of their own. Herzl promoted his ideas throughout Europe and the response, especially from eastern Europe and Russia, was so great that he organized the First Zionist Congress in Switzerland in 1897. At this meeting, the Zionist Organization was established and its goal was proclaimed—"to create for the Jewish people a home in Palestine secured by public law."[1]

In the following years, Herzl and the Zionist Organization sought international support for the goal of a Jewish homeland. Several other sites, including East Africa, were considered, but Palestine was chosen by the Zionists because it was the biblical homeland of the Jewish people. By 1914 Jews funded by the organization as well as various other private investors had established about forty settlements in Palestine, totaling approximately sixty thousand Jewish settlers. This new Jewish community in Palestine was called the "Yishuv," and was the beginning of a Jewish presence in Palestine that would grow larger after the end of Ottoman rule.

Conflicting British Promises

World War I resulted in the end of Ottoman rule over Palestine. At the outbreak of World War I in 1914, the Ottoman Empire entered the war on the side of Germany and became an enemy of Great Britain.

The British, hoping to sabotage Ottoman authority in the region, urged Palestinian Arabs to fight against their Ottoman rulers. In exchange for their loyalty, Britain promised the Arabs support for their independence after the war. These promises were contained in

Austrian Theodor Herzl founded the Zionist Organization, a group dedicated to creating a Jewish homeland in Palestine.

an informal series of letters between the British high commissioner in Egypt, Sir Henry McMahon, and Husayn ibn 'Ali, amir of Mecca and the most powerful Arab leader in Palestine. To fulfill his part of the bargain, Husayn, with support from British colonel T.E. Lawrence (popularly known as Lawrence of Arabia), organized attacks on Ottoman forces in Palestine. Later called the Arab Revolt, these attacks helped the British to defeat the Ottoman Empire.

Britain, however, had also made similar promises of support to Zionists in Palestine. Chaim Weizmann, an accomplished lecturer in chemistry in Britain, became a leader of the Zionist cause and met with various high-level British officials. He persuaded them to support Zionist goals. Largely as a result of Weizmann's efforts, the British foreign secretary, Arthur J. Balfour, sent a letter to Lord Lionel Rothschild, a British Zionist leader, expressing Britain's support for the creation of a Jewish homeland in Palestine. This letter, published on November 2, 1917, is called the Balfour Declaration.

At the same time as it was making promises to establish homelands in Palestine for both Arabs and Jews, Britain was making still other contradictory and secret agreements with its French, Russian, and Italian allies about how to divide up

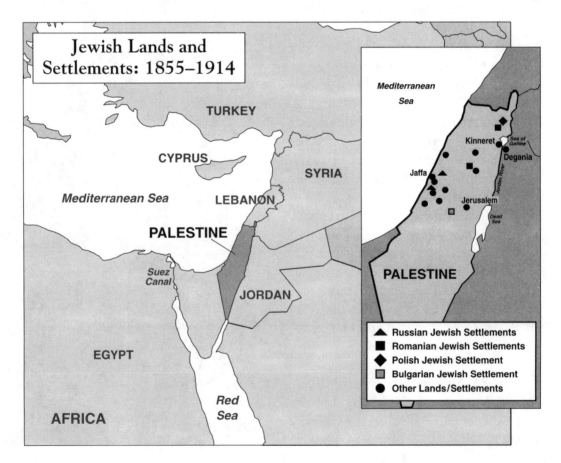

The Balfour Declaration

During World War I, Britain adopted a policy that favored the Zionist goal of establishing a home for Jews in Palestine. The policy, which became known as the Balfour Declaration, was articulated in a letter from British foreign secretary Arthur James Lord Balfour to Lord Rothschild, a Zionist leader. The letter, reprinted from the Israel Ministry of Foreign Affairs Web site, stated:

Dear Lord Rothschild,

I have much pleasure in conveying to you, on behalf of His Majesty's Government [the British government], the following declaration of sympathy with Jewish Zionist aspirations which has been submitted to, and approved by, the Cabinet.

"His Majesty's Government view with favour the establishment in Palestine of a national home for the Jewish people, and will use their best endeavours to facilitate the achievement of this object, it being clearly understood that nothing shall be done which may prejudice the civil and religious rights of existing non-Jewish communities in Palestine, or the rights and political status enjoyed by Jews in any other country."

I should be grateful if you would bring this declaration to the knowledge of the Zionist Federation.

Yours sincerely,

Arthur James Balfour

---

the Ottoman lands once Germany was defeated. Under the terms of the 1916 Sykes-Picot Agreement, for example, Ottoman lands in the areas surrounding Palestine were to be divided between Britain and France. Britain's various conflicting promises thus resulted in competing claims on Palestine and laid the groundwork for the Arab-Israeli conflict.

British Rule in Palestine

Even before the war ended, in December 1917, Britain had invaded and conquered Palestine, establishing a military occupation there. Britain had an interest in Palestine because it was an ideal base for defending other British colonies, such as India.

In 1919, after the war, the Allied nations of France, Great Britain, Russia, and the United States set up the King-Crane Commission to investigate the situation in Palestine and report back about the wishes of Palestinian Arabs. The commission was the idea of U.S. president Woodrow Wilson, who was then promoting national self-determination— the right of people to govern themselves. The commission concluded that Arabs wanted their own country and recommended independence for Palestine. Conversely, the commission recommended that the United States supervise Palestine and that the Zionist program be limited to slow the number of Jews immigrating to Palestine.

Instead of following the recommendations of the King-Crane Commission, however, the Allied powers met at a conference in San Remo, Italy, in April 1920 to decide the fate of Palestine. This conference, in a direct rejection of President Wilson's principle of self-determination, confirmed the division of lands agreed to in the Sykes-Picot Agreement, giving Britain control over Palestine. By approving British rule, the conference also renewed the principle of the Balfour Declaration, once again providing support for the Zionist dream of a Jewish homeland.

Britain's power over Palestine was confirmed in 1922 when it was granted a mandate by the League of Nations, an international body created after World War I to promote peace and security. Under the League's mandate system, countries such as Britain became trustees of former enemy territories in order to prepare them for self-rule. However, as Middle East analyst B. J. Smith explains, "the assignment of territory under the mandate system was little more than a thinly disguised title deed"[2] that gave Britain virtually complete control over the future of Palestine. In addition, the mandate explicitly encouraged Zionist settlement in Palestine and disregarded local Arab concerns. It recognized "the historical connection of the Jewish people with Palestine"[3] and instructed Britain to facilitate Jewish immigration. Arabs, however, who at that time con-

stituted approximately 90 percent of the population, were referred to by the mandate as "the other sections"[4] of the population.

Thereafter, apart from its encouragement of Jewish immigration, Britain treated Palestine as a typical British colony, controlling its trade, finances, and other economic policies.

Arab-Jewish Conflicts

Tensions between local Arabs and Jewish immigrants to Palestine arose in the 1880s with the establishment of the first Jewish settlements. Arguments often arose over issues such as grazing and land rights. As Arabs learned that the Zionist goal was to establish a Jewish homeland in Palestine, they became increasingly alarmed.

Following World War I, Arab frustrations were fueled by British rule over Palestine and continued Jewish immigration. Arab anger with the situation erupted in spontaneous demonstrations in various cities throughout the Middle East. In Palestine, tensions between Jews and Arabs escalated into not only political demonstrations but also riots and violence that resulted in many dead and wounded on both sides.

A British commission of inquiry appointed to investigate the causes of the violence concluded that it was due to the broken British promises of independence to Arabs and the attitude of the Zionists, which the report described as "arrogant, insolent and provocative." The report also contained a warning of future Arab-Jewish conflicts, stating that if the Zionists were "not carefully checked they may easily precipitate a catastrophe, the end of which it is difficult to forecast."[5]

Jewish Immigration Continues

The British, however, disregarded such warnings, choosing instead to support the Zionist cause by making land available to Jewish settlers, granting preferential treatment to Jews, and in other ways supporting the Jewish settlement movement. Britain's support for the Zionists was based on its belief that they could improve the area economically for both Jews and Arabs. As professor Samih K. Farsoun explains, Britain "saw the potential for economic growth of Palestine in the . . . Jewish immigrants with superior education, technological know-how, and capital that would produce an economic [prosperity] that would be shared with the poor and backward Palestinian Arabs."[6] With this economic growth, Britain believed Palestine could support a larger population and provide a home to both Jews and Arabs.

As a result, under the British mandate Jewish immigration to Palestine increased dramatically. Between 1919 and 1923, about thirty-five thousand Russian and eastern European Jews migrated to Palestine, followed by another wave of seventy-eight thousand Polish Jews between 1924 and 1928. Although this influx of educated and middle-class Jews

Jewish immigrants arrive in Palestine. Despite tensions between Arabs and Jews, immigration to Palestine continued during the 1920s.

helped to develop the area economically, creating jobs and opportunities for both Jews and local Arabs, Arabs remained opposed to the Jewish settlements and the policies of the Balfour Declaration. Indeed, in the early 1920s Arabs rejected British attempts to set up a legislative governing council that would have been comprised largely of Arabs, because they did not want to be part of the British mandate system at all.

In 1929 Jewish immigration increased further as a result of the worldwide economic depression and renewed anti-Semitism in Europe. Arabs once again rose up to resist the British occupation and Zionism. In August 1929, for example, rioting broke out in Jerusalem, Safed, and Hebron, and resulted in the death of 250 Arabs and Jews and the wounding of more than 500. Again, Britain responded by setting up an investigative commission, which found that Arabs were frustrated because they wanted independence and economic opportunities. Britain heeded the findings of this commission and in 1930 issued a statement, called the Passfield White Paper, halting Jewish immigration. As a result of political pressure from the Zionists, however, this statement was quickly reversed a year later by British prime minister James Ramsay MacDonald, again angering Arab groups.

The Arab Rebellion

By the early 1930s the rise of the Nazis in Germany and the subsequent anti-

The White Paper

Following the first Arab revolt against Britain in the late 1930s, Britain reevaluated its policy toward Jewish immigration to Palestine. The new policy, embodied in a document called the White Paper, abandoned the Balfour Declaration's support for Palestine as a homeland for the Jews. The White Paper, reprinted from Yale University's Web site, provided in part:

[1] The objective of His Majesty's Government [the British government] is the establishment within 10 years of an independent Palestine State. . . . The independent State should be one in which Arabs and Jews share government. . . .

[2] Jewish immigration during the next five years will . . . allow the admission, as from the beginning of April this year, of some 75,000 immigrants over the next five years. . . .

[3] After the period of five years, no further Jewish immigration will be permitted unless the Arabs of Palestine are prepared to [allow] it. [Britain's] purpose is to be just [fair] between the two people in Palestine whose destinies in that country have been affected by the great events of recent years, and who, since they live side by side, must learn to practice mutual tolerance, goodwill and cooperation.

Jewish policies there led to another large increase in Jewish immigration to Palestine, as thousands of German Jews fled Germany. By 1936 almost four hundred thousand Jews resided in Palestine, making up about 30 percent of the area's population and raising the possibility that Jews might one day outnumber native Arabs.

In response to the increasing numbers of Jewish settlements, the Arab community in Palestine organized a number of different groups, each opposed to Zionism. Some of these Arab groups began an armed struggle against both the British and the Jewish settlers, culminating in the first widespread Arab rebellion against British rule. The rebellion began in 1935 when the British killed Sheikh Izz ad-Din al-Qassam, a militant Arab religious leader who led a group of fighters in attacks on British troops. Following al-Qassam's murder, the sheikh became known as a hero, inspiring other Arab groups to continue the struggle.

Arabs later formed an Arab Higher Committee, which organized and directed a general strike that called for civil disobedience, refusal to pay taxes, and the shutdown of local governments. In addition, Arab militants made violent guerrilla attacks on government and Jewish targets, blowing up bridges, derailing trains, and seizing territory. The various Arab groups, however, disagreed about strategy and infighting broke out, resulting in many Arab deaths at the hands of other Arabs. Nevertheless, the rebellion was so effective and widespread that the British in 1938 were forced to send twenty thousand British troops to contain the violence. By the end of the rebellion in 1939, approximately 5,000 Arabs had been killed, 15,000 wounded, and another 5,600 imprisoned.

In addition to using force to suppress the uprising, the British set up another British commission, headed by Lord Robert Peel. The Peel Commission's report, in 1937, for the first time recommended that Palestine be divided into separate Jewish and Arab states. Jews accepted this idea of partition, but Palestinian Arabs rejected it, refusing to consider giving up any part of Palestine to the Jews. In hindsight, as journalist Ahron Bregman notes, this may have been a "grave error of judgment, for [the Arabs'] insistence on having all the land resulted . . . in their losing it all."[7]

Finally, Britain adopted a new policy, embodied in a document simply called the White Paper of May 1939. The White Paper proposed that Palestine become an independent state within ten years that would be governed by Arabs and Jews together. The White Paper also limited Jewish immigration to seventy-five thousand additional immigrants over a five-year period, and provided that after 1944 Arab consent would be necessary for any further immigration. This policy essentially ended the directives of the Balfour Declaration and reversed long-standing British policy on Jewish immigration.

After World War II broke out in 1939, attention shifted from the White Paper to the fight against Nazi Germany.

However, Jewish leaders such as David Ben-Gurion pledged to continue the battle for a Jewish homeland, stating, "We shall fight the war as if there were no White Paper; we shall fight the White Paper as if there were no war!"[8]

Jewish Resistance Against British Rule

World War II and the murder of 6 million Jews by the Nazis in what became known as the Holocaust made the Zionist movement even more committed to building a Jewish homeland in Palestine. As historians Ian J. Bickerton and Carla L. Klausner explain, "For the world's Jews . . . the Holocaust created an irresistible sense that something should be done in Palestine to atone for the Holocaust and to compensate the remnants of European Jewry."[9] Despite the tragedy of the Jews who suffered and died at the hands of the Nazis, however, Britain continued to implement the White Paper and restrict Jewish immigration throughout the war and even after the war ended. The British actions prevented thousands of Jewish war refugees from getting to Palestine.

As a result of these policies, Jews during the war organized a campaign to resist British rule. Yishuv leaders had formed an illegal underground fighting force called the Haganah during the 1936–1939 Arab rebellion, and later some more militant Haganah members broke away to form an organization called the Irgun Zvai Leumi. Another paramilitary group led by Avraham Stern, called Fighters for the Freedom of Israel (known as Lehi or the Stern Gang), broke away from the Irgun. Both Irgun and the Stern Gang became known as terrorist groups due to their ruthless tactics and their willingness to kill British soldiers and civilians manning British government offices. By the war's end, the Haganah had joined with the Irgun and the Stern Gang and all three groups participated in attacks on British installations set up to suppress Jewish immigration.

After the war ended in May 1945, the Allied powers were faced with finding homes for about 7 million refugees, many of them Jewish. Jewish groups worked to help many of these refugees immigrate to Palestine illegally. Britain opposed these efforts, resulting in an escalation of Yishuv violence against British targets. Jewish attacks struck British military headquarters and offices and blew up bridges and railways, destroying transportation lines. For example, in 1946, Jewish Irgun terrorists blew up the King David Hotel, where British headquarters were located, killing close to a hundred people.

As the violence in Palestine mounted, Britain became increasingly motivated to find a solution and wash its hands of the problem. Several efforts to resolve the issue failed. Amid increasing violence in Palestine between Jewish militants and British troops, and growing cost to the already struggling British economy, Britain finally decided to abandon Palestine. Accordingly, in January 1947, Britain turned the matter over to the United Nations, a new international organization created after World War II to replace the League of Nations.

The Irgun

During World War II the Jews in Palestine, who wanted their own government in Palestine, instituted a campaign of terrorism against British rule. The group that led this terrorist effort was the Irgun, headed by Menachem Begin, who later became prime minister of Israel.

In the early 1940s the British adamantly adhered to their "White Paper" policy of not allowing further immigration of Jews to Israel, despite the emerging news about the Holocaust and Germany's extermination of Jews in Europe. In response, beginning in 1943 the Irgun undertook a series of brutal attacks against the British.

In one well-known incident, the Irgun in 1946 bombed the main British government headquarters in the King David Hotel in Jerusalem, killing ninety British, Arab, and Jewish workers. Other attacks by the Irgun included the bombing of British immigration offices, intelligence centers, and police stations, and transportation sites such as bridges and railroads. The Jews, with the help of Irgun and other Jewish guerrilla groups, ultimately succeeded in ousting the British from Israel, and in 1947 the United Nations voted to partition Palestine and create a separate Jewish state. Israel declared its independence the following year.

British soldiers attend to casualties of the 1946 King David Hotel bombing.

The Birth of Israel

The issue of Palestine was one of the first problems taken up by the UN. A UN Special Committee on Palestine (UNSCOP), after numerous hearings, unanimously recommended that the British mandate over Palestine be terminated and that Palestine be granted independence following a two-year transition period during which Britain would retain control. The majority of UNSCOP members recommended partition of Palestine into a Jewish state and an Arab state, with Jerusalem as an international city. A minority, however, thought partition was unworkable and proposed that Palestine be kept united as a collection of self-governing Arab and Jewish states.

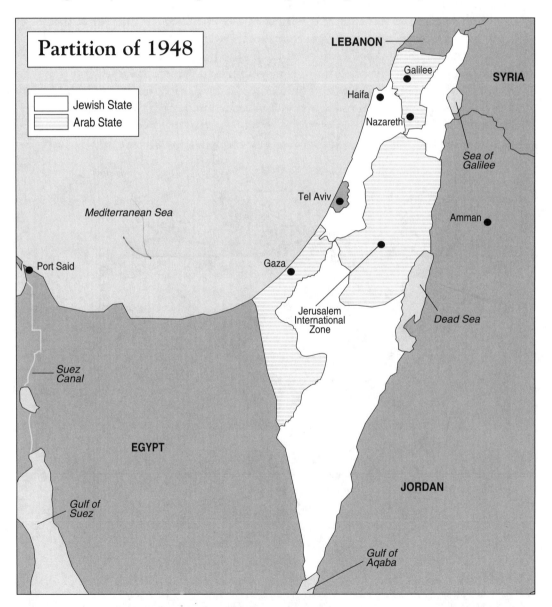

Partition of 1948

Jewish State
Arab State

LEBANON

Galilee

Haifa

Nazareth

SYRIA

Sea of Galilee

Mediterranean Sea

Tel Aviv

Amman

Gaza

Port Said

Jerusalem International Zone

Dead Sea

Suez Canal

EGYPT

JORDAN

Gulf of Suez

Gulf of Aqaba

Jewish leaders accepted UNSCOP's majority recommendation for partition, but Arabs rejected both the majority and minority reports, and the Arab League threatened war if the United Nations accepted either report. The British took no position on the future of Palestine. Instead, Britain announced that it would abandon its mandate early, effective May 14, 1948, leaving the decision on Palestine up to the United Nations.

Meanwhile, the British were left to deal with the violence and continuing illegal immigration. One famous case involved a ship called the *Exodus 1947*, carrying about forty-five hundred Jewish refugees. The ship sailed from France to Palestine, but before arrival, was rammed and boarded by the British and several refugees were killed in the ensuing fight. The rest were transferred to deportation ships bound for France.

The UN General Assembly on November 29, 1947, voted to partition Palestine. UN Resolution 181 was supported by thirty-three countries, including the United States, but it was strenuously opposed by all Islamic countries. Britain did not vote. Sympathy for the post-Holocaust tragedy of the Jews produced a plan under which the Jews, who made up about 31 percent of the Palestinian population, were awarded 55 per-cent of the land, while Arabs were given 45 percent.

For the Jews, therefore, the UN vote was a great victory. For the Arabs, however, it was devastating news. In their disappointment, Arab groups decided not to accept partition of Palestine, even though it would have created an independent Palestinian nation. It was a decision that many today believe was a huge mistake. Instead, the Arabs declared a general strike, and civil war broke out in Palestine between the Arab Liberation Army, armed by Syria, and the Jewish Haganah. The war produced atrocities on both sides. For example, in April 1948, members of the Irgun and Stern Gang attacked a small Arab village near Jerusalem called Deir Yassin, reportedly raped girls and women, and killed most of the villagers—about 254 men, women, and children. Days later, Palestinian Arabs attacked a Jewish medical team, killing seventy-seven.

This chaos continued until May 14, 1948, when Britain officially terminated the mandate and abruptly pulled its forces out of Palestine. At 4:00 P.M. that same day, Israel declared its independence and eleven minutes later, the United States recognized the new country, giving it legitimacy. In this painful way, the nation of Israel was born.

BOONE COUNTY
4248293

CHAPTER 2

The Arab-Israeli Wars

Following Israel's birth in 1948, the new country fought a series of wars with Palestinian Arabs and surrounding Arab states. The first of these Arab-Israeli wars occurred immediately after Israel declared its independence, when neighboring Arab states sent their armies to attack the Jewish nation. Israel won this 1948 War of Independence but it was a tragedy for Palestinians. It became the first of many struggles between Israelis and Arabs, creating a climate of war that would last beyond the next five decades.

The War of Independence and Its Refugees

On May 15, 1948, the day after Israel announced its independence, five Arab states—Egypt, Jordan, Syria, Lebanon, and Iraq—invaded Israel to help the Arab Liberation Army and the Palestin-ian Arabs destroy the new country. The ensuing war became known in Israel as the War of Independence, but Palestinians call it *al-Nakba* or "the disaster."[10]

At the start of the war Arabs quickly gained inroads into parts of Israel. In June, however, a mediator appointed by the United Nations, Count Folke Bernadotte, arranged for a month-long truce in hope of finding a peaceful settlement. During this time Israel organized and built up its military forces, and when fighting resumed, Israeli forces took the offensive, retaking much of the territory seized by Arab troops before the cease-fire. On September 16 Bernadotte recommended a peace plan to the United Nations but Israel strongly opposed the plan, and the very next day Bernadotte was assassinated by the Jewish terrorist group, the Stern Gang.

Hostilities continued for several more months, but Israel prevailed due to its organized command structure, its modern weapons, and most of all, its fierce determination to win what it viewed as a battle for its very existence. For Jews who had just lived through the Holocaust, this war was another fight against extermination.

In contrast, the Arab forces were disorganized, unprepared, outmanned, and divided in their motives. For example, King Abdullah of Jordan was more interested in acquiring Palestinian land for Jordan than in defending the Palestinians; indeed, after the war, both Jordan and Egypt seized remaining Palestinian areas for themselves, disregarding Palestinian desires for an independent state. The war's end finally came in February 1949, when Egypt and Israel signed an armistice, followed by armistice agreements with Lebanon, Jordan, and Syria. Iraq withdrew its troops but refused to sign an armistice with Israel.

Israel had won its first war and had clearly proved it was strong enough militarily to defend itself. Indeed, Israel seized and held not only all of the territory awarded to it by the United Nations but additional Palestinian territory as well. For Palestinians, therefore, the war

Israeli soldiers lead an assault on Egyptian troops during the 1948 War of Independence.

meant the creation of an expanded Jewish state beyond the areas awarded under the UN partition plan. In addition, because Jordan and Egypt snatched other Palestinian areas such as East Jerusalem and Gaza, the Palestinians were left with essentially no land they could call their own.

Even worse, the war created about 750,000 Palestinian refugees, who fled from their homes in the territories conquered by Israel to other Arab countries and parts of Palestine that came under Arab control. Middle East historian Rashid Khalidi describes the devastating effect of the war on Palestinians:

> Between early spring and late fall of 1948, Arab Palestine was radically transformed. . . . Over this turbulent period, more than half of the nearly 1.4 million Palestinian Arabs were driven from or fled their homes. Those Palestinians who did not flee the conquered areas were reduced to a small minority within the new state of Israel. At the end of the fighting, Jordan took over the areas of Palestine controlled by its army west of the Jordan River, while the Egyptian army administered the strip it retained around Gaza, adjacent to its borders. In the wake of this catastrophe—al-Nakba, as it was inscribed in Palestinian memory—the Palestinians found themselves living under a variety of alien regimes, were dispossessed of the vast bulk of their property, and had lost control over most aspects of their lives.[11]

This terrible loss and the resulting Palestinian refugee problem would fuel deep Arab anger and become a major issue in the Arab-Israeli conflict for years to come.

The 1956 Suez-Sinai War

Following the 1948 war Israel devoted itself to stabilizing its government and economy and absorbing hundreds of thousands of new Jewish immigrants. Indeed, one of the first actions taken by the new Israeli government was to pass the Law of Return, which provided that Jews from anywhere in the world could immigrate to Israel and be granted automatic citizenship. Many Palestinian Arabs, on the other hand, were primarily concerned with physical survival in their newfound refugee status.

However, a few Palestinian individuals and small groups continued to make raids into Israel, sometimes killing Israelis. Israel responded with retaliatory attacks into Arab lands with regular army forces, and a cycle of raids and retaliatory strikes began.

One Israeli attack in 1955 on an Egyptian military post in Gaza killed thirty-eight Egyptians and wounded another sixty-two. It marked a turning point in Egyptian-Israeli relations, inspiring Egypt to prepare for war. In response to the Israeli raid on Gaza, Egypt set up commando training camps to train Palestinian refugees in guerrilla tactics (unconventional warfare tactics such as sabotage, harassment, and hit-and-run fighting). These fighters, called fedayeen, were then encouraged by Egypt to attack Israel. In addition, Egypt led an economic boycott against Israel, closed two waterways—the Suez Canal

The Palestinian Refugees

The creation of Israel in 1948 and the ensuing civil war between Israelis and Arabs in Palestine caused a mass exodus of Palestinian Arabs to refugee camps in neighboring Arab states. Approximately 750,000 Palestinians, or about 75 percent of the native Arab population in Palestine, fled their homeland or were forced out, never to be allowed back. The exodus began shortly after the United Nations voted to partition Palestine into separate Jewish and Arab states, and it escalated during the 1948 war, especially after word spread about a Jewish massacre of civilians in the Arab village of Deir Yassin in April 1948. The 1967 Six-Day War, in which Israel seized additional Arab lands, produced about 300,000 more Palestinian refugees.

The refugees are still a problem today. Indeed, it is estimated that there are now about 2.5 million registered Palestinian refugees living in thirty-two refugee camps located in Jordan, Syria, and Lebanon. Although called camps, the areas are better described as slums. The right of these refugees to return to their Palestinian homeland is one of the thorny issues that has been debated, but not resolved, during peace negotiations between Israel and the Palestinians.

and Gulf of Aqaba—to Israeli ships, and built up its military, causing Israel to fear that Egypt might attack at any time.

Finally, in 1956, Egypt's president, Gamal Abdel Nasser, nationalized the Suez Canal, an action that soon led to war with not only Israel but also Britain and France. The Suez Canal is a key trade waterway in Egypt connecting the Mediterranean Sea with the Red Sea. It had been declared neutral territory, guaranteeing free passage to all in time of peace and war. It was operated by the Suez Canal Company, whose major shareholders were France and Britain, under an agreement with Egypt. Nasser, however, claiming Egypt needed the income from the canal, took over the company (but offered to pay the two countries the value of their shares). Nasser's action angered both France, which had already had its differences with Egypt over Egypt's support for rebels in French Algeria, and Britain, which depended on access to the canal to reach its oil interests in the Persian Gulf. Britain and France therefore hatched a plan to attack Nasser, with Israel's help, in order to regain control of the Suez Canal.

On October 29, 1956, Israel, supported by France and Britain, launched a coordinated attack on Egypt, hoping to destroy the fedayeen and at the same time topple Nasser from power and reopen the Suez Canal. The Israeli attack began with a paratroop drop that completely surprised the Egyptians, followed quickly by British and French air attacks on Egyptian air bases. By the time a cease-fire was agreed to a month later, Israel had easily conquered and seized large parts of Palestine controlled by Egypt, including Gaza and all of the

Sinai desert up to the Suez Canal. Israel was again victorious over the Arabs, and this time over Egypt, the strongest Arab nation in the world.

The following year, 1957, the Suez Canal was reopened and due to international pressure Israel was forced by the United Nations to withdraw from Sinai and Gaza. As a result, although defeated and humiliated militarily, Nasser regained all of Egypt's territory and became known in the Arab world as a hero who stood up against Zionism. Even in defeat, Nasser maintained that the Arab goal was the eventual destruction of Israel. Like earlier conflicts, therefore, the Suez-Sinai War only served to inflame Arab-Israeli tensions.

Egyptian president Gamel Abdel Nasser parades through Cairo in 1956 after announcing that he had nationalized the Suez Canal.

The 1967 Six-Day War

In the decade following the 1956 war, Israel continued to grow as an independent country, making impressive economic, political, and cultural gains. Israel's economic growth resulted in a need for increased water resources for its agriculture and industry, and in 1956 Israel began a construction project to divert water from the Sea of Galilee, a lake in Israel fed by the Jordan River. The Arab states opposed this project; they did not want Israel to grow or use up precious water resources. As the project was nearing completion in 1964, the Arab states met in Cairo, Egypt, and agreed to erect dams on tributary rivers to divert water from the Jordan River, thereby reducing the amount of water available to the Sea of Galilee and to Israel. However, after the Israeli military attacked the construction project, it was abandoned. This caused increasing friction on the Syrian-Israeli border, leading to sporadic gunfights between the Syrian and Israeli armies, as well as concern among other Arab states.

Meanwhile, after the 1956 war Egyptian president Nasser became a leader in the Arab world, promoting an anti-Western, pro-Arab philosophy that became known as pan-Arabism. This philosophy sought to unite Arab countries to increase their political and military power and boost Arab pride. As part of this philosophy, Egypt, Syria, and Jordan in 1966 and 1967 formed pacts to support each other militarily in case of war. In addition, believing that Israel's goal was to expand into additional parts of Palestine, Nasser rebuilt his military

in preparation for future conflicts with Israel. He obtained weapons from the Soviet Union, which was anxious to form ties with countries in the Middle East.

Nasser's growing relationship with the Soviets, in turn, caused the United States to begin supplying arms to Israel in order to counter Soviet influence in the Middle East. Over time, as tensions increased between the United States and the Soviet Union in what became known as the Cold War, both countries began sending massive arms shipments to various Middle East countries—with U.S. arms going to Israel, Iran, and Saudi Arabia, and Soviet weapons going to Egypt, Syria, and Iraq. The presence of such weapons in a volatile area like the Middle East made conditions ripe for conflict.

In early May 1967, as the border fighting between Syria and Israel escalated, Egypt's ally, the Soviet Union, notified Egypt that Israel had heavy troop concentrations on the Syrian-Israeli border and that Israel planned to attack Syria. Though this information later proved to be false, it caused Nasser to send Egyptian troops to the Israeli border and to once again close the Gulf of Aqaba to Israeli ships or ships carrying goods to Israel. Israel viewed Nasser's actions as acts of aggression and decided to strike against Egypt before it could attack Israel.

On June 5, 1967, in a sensational surprise attack, Israel destroyed most of Egypt's air force, which comprised over four hundred planes. At the same time, Israel attacked Egyptian ground forces

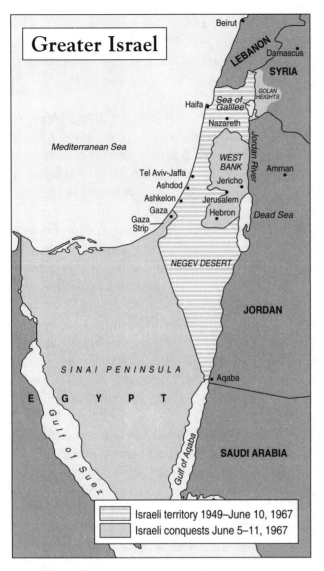

Greater Israel

Beirut
LEBANON
Damascus
SYRIA
GOLAN
HEIGHTS
Haifa
Sea of
Galilee
Nazareth
Mediterranean Sea
WEST
BANK
Jordan River
Tel Aviv-Jaffa
Amman
Ashdod
Jericho
Ashkelon
Jerusalem
Gaza
Hebron
Gaza
Dead Sea
Strip
NEGEV DESERT
JORDAN
SINAI PENINSULA
Aqaba
E   G   Y   P   T
Gulf of Suez
Gulf of Aqaba
SAUDI ARABIA

Israeli territory 1949–June 10, 1967
Israeli conquests June 5–11, 1967

rael advanced into Syrian territory and captured the Golan Heights. By June 10, 1967, six days after the start of the war, the Israelis had achieved a spectacular victory.

Israel had firmly established its military dominance in the Middle East and captured multiple new Arab territories—Gaza, the Sinai peninsula, all of Jerusalem, the West Bank, and the Golan Heights. As historians Ian J. Bickerton and Carla L. Klausner explain, "A new map of the Middle East came into being, with Israel three times larger than it was in 1949."[12] The newly occupied areas provided economic benefits for Israel, such as the Sinai oil fields, and created a buffer between Israel and surrounding Arab states, reducing the danger of a surprise Arab attack. Israel's seizure of Arab lands, however, also created more than three hundred thousand new Palestinian refugees, further incensed the defeated Arab countries, and fueled support for the Palestinian cause.

and, for the second time, captured the Sinai and Gaza. Although the Arabs were well-supplied with weapons and equipment, Israel's organized army and air force dramatically defeated Egyptian forces in three days' time. Next, when Jordan became involved in the war, Israel destroyed Jordan's air bases and seized the Jordanian-held territories of Jerusalem and the entire West Bank. Finally, although the United Nations called for a cease-fire, Is-

The War of Attrition

The Arab world viewed the 1967 war as another disaster, comparable to the 1948 war with Israel. Arab countries met at an Arab League summit in September 1967 and declared that there could be no peace with Israel, no negotiations, and no recognition. The league called on the United Nations to order Israel to withdraw from the territories occupied during the war. Instead, the United Nations on November 22, 1967, adopted Resolution 242, a land-for-peace compromise, which stated that Israel should withdraw from all occupied territories and that Arabs, in return, should recognize the right of Israel to live in peace. Israel accepted the resolution, as did Egypt and Jordan, signifying implicitly for the first time their willingness to accept Israel's existence as a nation and the need for a negotiated solution to the Israeli-Arab dispute.

Tensions quickly reappeared between Egypt and Israel, however, leading to a border war between the two countries that later became known as the War of Attrition. Egypt, equipped with a new supply of Soviet weapons, fired artillery into Israeli outposts along the border. Israel responded by bombing Egyptian towns and cities in the Suez Canal zone.

Eventually, the United States was successful in negotiating a solution. Called the Rogers Plan after U.S. secretary of state William Rogers, the peace plan called for a ninety-day cease-fire, Israeli withdrawal from the occupied territories in exchange for recognition, and UN mediation efforts. A cease-fire went into effect in August 1970, but peace negotiations soon dissolved, and Israeli occupation of the territories—including Gaza, the Sinai peninsula, Jerusalem, the West Bank, and the Golan Heights— continued. In addition, for the first time, Jewish settlements slowly began to appear in many of these territories.

The Growth of Palestinian Guerrilla Groups

The 1967 war, Israel's occupation of Palestinian territories, and the failure of UN-sponsored peace efforts led to growing Palestinian frustration as well as an increasing sense of Palestinian identity. Palestinians had previously relied on neighboring Arab governments to protect them from Israel, but that had clearly failed and so they began to turn to their own leaders. Indeed, Palestinian groups began to form as early as 1964, when the Palestine Liberation Organization (PLO) was created by the Arab League. In addition, a Palestine Liberation Army (PLA) was formed to liberate Palestine from Israel through armed struggle. Initially, therefore, the PLO was the creation of the Arab states and was dependent upon them for its funding. Its first leader was Ahmad Shuqayri, a former lawyer and spokesperson for various Arab governments.

In addition, a second, more independent Palestinian group, called al-Fatah (meaning conquest), emerged at this time. Although al-Fatah was founded earlier by Palestinian students living in Egypt (including Yasir Arafat), in the 1960s the group became allied with Syria and grew more active. Even before the 1967 war, while the Syrian army fought with the Israeli army on the Syrian-Israeli border, al-Fatah conducted guerrilla raids into Israel, from both Syrian and Jordanian territory. Other Palestinian guerrilla groups also appeared and joined al-Fatah in guerrilla raids against Israeli targets.

Because wars between Arab and Israeli military forces had only worsened the plight of Palestinians, these new Palestinian leaders believed that armed guerrilla struggle by the Palestinian people was the only way to undermine Israel and liberate Palestine from Jewish occupation. Accordingly, after the 1967 war, the various Palestinian resistance groups established underground bases within the occupied territories and carried out attacks against Israel from both these bases and bases within Jordan. These attacks were highly publicized and helped build mass support for the Palestinian cause within the Arab community.

One incident in July 1968 had particular meaning for Palestinians. It occurred when Israeli forces attacked al-Karameh, a Palestinian guerrilla base in Jordan, and Palestinian fighters with the help of the Jordanian army repelled the attack and inflicted heavy Israeli casualties. Because Palestinian guerrilla fighters stayed to fight against superior Israeli troops instead of withdrawing, as guerrilla fighters often do, al-Karameh became a heroic symbol for the new Palestinian resistance. As sociologist Samih K. Farsoun explains, "In Arabic the noun *al-karameh* means dignity, and the battle was seen as the beginning of the restoration of Arab dignity after the humiliating defeat of the Six-Day War."[13]

"The Sole Representative of the Palestinians"

By 1968 the PLO ceased to be a group controlled by the Arab governments and became a true leader of the Palestinian resistance movement. Shuqayri resigned as leader of the PLO and was replaced by a charismatic young leader named Yasir Arafat. The PLO then became the representative for many other Palestinian guerrilla groups, with each group retaining a significant amount of autonomy.

Groups working with the PLO included al-Fatah, the Popular Front for the Liberation of Palestine (PFLP), the PFLP–General Command, the Democratic Front for the Liberation of Palestine (DFLP), the Palestine Resistance Movement (PRM), and the Palestine People's Party (PPP). Only two groups—the radical group Hamas and a smaller group called Islamic Jihad—refused to join the PLO framework.

Thereafter, the PLO reorganized and by the mid-1970s began providing services and protection to Palestinian refugees and Palestinians in occupied areas. In addition, the PLO continued guerrilla strikes against Israel and engaged in terrorist activities designed to gain international attention and support for the Palestinian cause. Two of the most infamous incidents of terrorism associated with the PLO, for example, included a 1968 hijacking of an Israeli airliner and the murder of eleven Israeli athletes during the 1972 Munich Olympic Games.

The PLO grew so strong, in fact, that it began to threaten Arab countries that had been providing it safe haven. King Hussein I of Jordan, where the PLO was headquartered, in 1970 launched a campaign to drive the PLO guerrillas out of his country. Jordan's ouster of the PLO caused Palestinian militants to scale back some of their terrorist activities. It also forced them to move PLO operations into southern Lebanon and establish their headquarters in Beirut.

The PLO's international prestige also increased dramatically during the 1970s.

Terrorist or Freedom Fighter?

On November 13, 1974, in a speech excerpted below from a reprint in the Journal of Palestinian Studies, *Yasir Arafat, leader of the Palestine Liberation Organization (PLO) made a dramatic appearance before the UN General Assembly and called on the world community to view the PLO not as terrorists but as freedom fighters resisting Israeli occupation and oppression. Arafat declared:*

The difference between the revolutionary and the terrorist lies in the reason for which each fights. Whoever stands by a just cause and fights for liberation from invaders and colonialists cannot be called terrorist. Those who wage war to occupy, colonize and oppress other people are the terrorists. . . . The Palestinian people had to resort to armed struggle when they lost faith in the international community, which ignored their rights, and when it became clear that not one inch of Palestine could be regained through exclusively political means. . . . The PLO dreams and hopes for one democratic state where Christian, Jew and Muslim live in justice, equality, fraternity and progress. The chairman of the PLO and leader of the Palestinian revolution appeals to the General Assembly to accompany the Palestinian people in its struggle to attain its right of self-determination. . . . I have come bearing an olive branch and a freedom fighter's gun. Do not let the olive branch fall from my hand.

The appearance of Arafat before the United Nations was a diplomatic victory for the PLO. Nine days after Arafat's speech, the United Nations voted to grant the PLO observer status and to give international recognition to the Palestinian peoples' right to self-determination.

Yasir Arafat addresses the United Nations in November 1974.

During the 1973 Arab summit, for example, the Arab states recognized the PLO as the "sole representative of the Palestinians."[14] In 1974 the United Nations also recognized the PLO as the Palestinian representative, invited Yassir Arafat to speak to the UN assembly, and adopted a resolution affirming Palestinians' right to self-determination and independence.

The 1973 Yom Kippur War

In 1970 Egyptian president Nasser died suddenly of a heart attack and was succeeded by then vice president Anwar el-Sadat. He quickly began a campaign to redeem Egypt from its 1967 defeat by seeking Israel's withdrawal from some of the territories seized in the Six-Day War.

First, beginning in 1971 Sadat tried diplomacy, offering a cease-fire, diplomatic relations with the United States, reopening of the Suez Canal, and a peace agreement with Israel if Israel would withdraw from parts of the Sinai Peninsula. Israel, however, refused to give up land it claimed it had won in war. Sadat then decided to regain Egypt's lost territory by force.

On October 6, 1973, Egyptian and Syrian forces launched a surprise attack on Israel on Yom Kippur, Judaism's most somber and holy day. The war resulted in some of the heaviest fighting since World War II and became known in Israel as the Yom Kippur War. To Arabs it was known as the Ramadan War, because it occurred during Ramadan, a holy

The 1973 Oil Embargo

One of the results of the Yom Kippur War between Egypt and Israel was an oil embargo and a worldwide recession. On October 17, 1973, the Organization of Arab Oil-Producing Countries (OAPEC) imposed a total embargo on oil exports to the United States. OAPEC's action was made in support of Egypt and to punish the United States for its support of Israel. OAPEC also placed embargos of various degrees on other countries, depending on the amount of their support for Israel. Two months later, the Organization of Petroleum Exporting Countries (OPEC), to which OAPEC members belonged, announced a fourfold increase in the price of oil. This was the first time in history that Arab countries used oil as a political weapon.

The oil embargo disrupted the world economy and caused a worldwide recession that was felt in the United States and in countries around the world. The embargo reportedly cost the United States five hundred thousand jobs and a $10 billion to $20 billion loss in its gross national product, an economic indicator that measures economic output. For the Arabs, the embargo was a political success. It was ended only after diplomacy produced agreements between Israel and Egypt, and Israel and Syria, which provided for Israel to return certain Syrian and Egyptian lands it had seized during the war.

An Israeli soldier leads blindfolded Egyptian POWs captured during the 1973 Yom Kippur War.

month for Muslims. Israel, with an infusion of U.S. arms, eventually beat back the attack and won the war, but Arabs showed they could plan and execute a secret and effective attack, thereby redeeming much of their lost honor. The war ended with a cease-fire negotiated by the United States and the Soviet Union and approved by the United Nations in Resolution 338, which called on the parties to begin direct peace negotiations. Over the next couple of years, U.S. secretary of state Henry Kissinger pursued a step-by-step peace approach that by 1975 persuaded Israel to return Egyptian and Syrian lands it had seized during the war and restore oil installations to Egypt. Egypt in return opened the Suez Canal for ships delivering goods to and from Israel.

In the end, although Israel won militarily, Egypt emerged from the war with a psychological victory. Egypt had shown that Arabs could wage war effectively and that Israel was not completely invincible. Although Arab losses were also great, the war cost Israel over twenty-eight hundred soldiers' lives, eighty-five hundred wounded, and about one-third of Israel's total budget for 1973. For these reasons, it became clear to both Arabs and Israelis that continued warfare was detrimental to all, leading to an era of peace initiatives between Arabs and Israelis.

CHAPTER 3

The Palestinians Rise Up

The decade following the 1973 war was marked by efforts on Egypt's part to find a peaceful solution to the Arab-Israeli standoff, as well as by growing Palestinian dissatisfaction and unrest when peace efforts failed to bring an acceptable solution for them. Egypt finally gave up on the Palestinian cause and made a separate peace with Israel, while Israel hardened its stance toward the Palestinian territories and built more settlements. These two developments led Palestinians to the brink of hopelessness and despair, which took the form of increased Palestinian resistance against Israel. This culminated in a widespread, grassroots Palestinian uprising against the occupation and Israeli policies that became known as the first "intifada."

Israel Encourages Settlements

The surprise attack that led to the 1973 Yom Kippur War caused many Israelis to question Israeli leadership, which had been dominated by the politically moderate Labor Party. As a result, four years later, in May 1977, Israelis elected the opposition Likud Party into office, making Menachem Begin Israel's new prime minister.

This victory marked a major shift in Israeli politics. The Labor Party had favored the idea of giving up occupied land for peace. Likud, however, favored a policy of retaining Israeli control over the occupied territories. In line with Likud priorities, after his election Begin immediately began to encourage expanded Jewish settlements in the West Bank and other occupied territories. He believed that the establishment of settlements in the territories was Israel's right; it was their land, he argued, and thus Israeli citizens had a right to build on it. Also, the more people, homes, businesses, and services became established in the territories, the harder it would be for anyone to ask Israel to withdraw from the land. In other words, the development of settlements would create a new set of realities that would reduce the chance that Israel would later have to withdraw from the territories.

For example, in December 1977 Begin proclaimed: "We do not even dream of the possibility . . . of abandoning these [occupied] areas to the control of the murderous organization that is called the PLO. . . . We have a right and a demand for [Israeli] sovereignty over these areas. . . . This is our land and it belongs to the Jewish nation rightfully."[15] As a result of Begin's policies, by 1981 the number of Jewish settlers in the occupied lands rose to about 110,000.

Sadat's Peace Initiative and the Camp David Accords

Meanwhile, Egyptian president Sadat had become less concerned with the Palestinians than with the cost to Egypt of maintaining a hostile stance toward Israel. Indeed, Sadat surprised the world in 1977 by offering to personally fly to Israel to discuss peace in the first-ever face-to-face negotiations between Arabs and Israelis. Sadat became interested in making a deal with Israel after riots broke out in Egypt over food prices, because peace would allow him to reduce military expenditures and focus on economic rebuilding.

Sadat's Speech to the Israeli Knesset

Egyptian president Anwar el-Sadat became the first Arab leader to meet directly with Israel when he flew to Israel in November 1977. Sadat's November 20, 1977, speech to the Israeli Knesset (parliament) is excerpted below from a reprint in Ahron Bregman and Jihan el-Tahri's The Fifty Years' War:

I come to you today on solid ground to shape a new life and to establish peace. Any life that is lost is a human life, be it that of an Arab or an Israeli. . . . Conceive with me a peace agreement . . . based on the following points: Ending the occupation of the Arab territories occupied in 1967. . . . Achievement of the fundamental rights of the Palestinian people and their right of self-determination, including their right to establish their own state. The right of all states in the area to live in peace. . . . You, sorrowing mother, you, widowed wife, you, the son who lost a brother or a father, all the victims of wars, fill the air and space with recitals of peace, fill bosoms and hearts with aspiration of peace.

Sadat's initiative started peace negotiations between Egypt and Israel that resulted in the 1977 Camp David Accords, which returned the Sinai to Egypt and produced a peace treaty between Egypt and Israel. Sadat's actions, however, angered other Arab states, Palestinians, and many Egyptians. On October 6, 1981, he paid for peace with his life when he was assassinated by Egyptian Muslim extremists opposed to the peace treaty.

Israeli prime minister Menachem Begin (left), American president Jimmy Carter (center), and Egyptian president Anwar Sadat convene for the Camp David Accords in 1978.

Israeli prime minister Begin, known as a hard-line politician, surprisingly responded to Sadat's offer with an invitation, and on November 19, Sadat flew to Israel and addressed the Israeli parliament, called the Knesset. The moment was historic; it was the first time Arab and Israeli leaders had directly and publicly met since the creation of Israel twenty-nine years before. In the dramatic speech, Sadat presented his peace plan and told Israelis that Egypt wanted to live with Israel in a permanent peace.

Following Sadat's visit to Israel, the two sides began U.S.-chaperoned peace negotiations. In September 1978 U.S. president Jimmy Carter invited Begin and Sadat to come to his presidential retreat in Camp David, Maryland. The meeting produced two accords, or agreements, which later came to be known as the Camp David Accords. Under these agreements, Israel was to allow a self-governing, elected Palestinian authority to operate in the West Bank and Gaza, two of the areas seized from Arabs by Israel in 1967. In addition, the accords required Israel to withdraw from all of the Sinai, the Egyptian territory seized by Israel. In exchange, Egypt agreed to establish normal relations with Israel and guarantee Israeli ships unrestricted use of the Suez Canal. On March 26, 1979, Sadat and Begin signed an Egyptian-Israeli peace treaty that is still in effect today.

The Camp David Accords marked a major turn in the Arab-Israeli conflict, but they fell short of establishing a comprehensive peace settlement in several respects. Most importantly, they did not provide for a separate, independent Palestinian state, a concession many considered key to a lasting peace but one that Begin would not consider. In addition, the accords did not settle how to deal with other Israeli-occupied lands in Jerusalem and the Golan Heights, and left the issue of how to transition to self-governance in the West Bank and Gaza somewhat vague. Finally, while they provided a separate peace for Egypt, allowing it to rebound economically, the Camp David Accords did not include a peace deal with other Arab countries that still posed a threat to Israel's security, such as Jordan, Syria, and Lebanon. Indeed, the Arab League, angry over the accords, met shortly after the accords were signed to impose political and economic sanctions against Egypt and suspend it from the league.

Palestinian Unrest

Palestinians were also not satisfied with the Camp David Accords. They sought an independent Palestinian state, which was very different from the self-rule plan negotiated by Egypt at Camp David. As the realities of the self-rule plan emerged, Palestinians became even more disgruntled. Israel clearly intended to limit the amount of authority granted to the Palestinians and squelched any idea that the accords would lead to an Israeli withdrawal from the West Bank and Gaza.

Instead, Israel dramatically increased the number of Jewish settlements in occupied areas, especially in the West Bank. Israel also exercised its control over those areas by increasing its military presence and taking control of water resources. It became increasingly clear that Israeli policies had not really changed, and that, despite the return of the Sinai to Egypt, Begin intended to stick to his principle of not giving up any other occupied lands to Palestinian control. Given this context, negotiations between Egypt and Israel to set up a process for achieving Palestinian self-rule in the territories stalled, and in 1980 Sadat suspended the talks.

Palestinian groups responded to the deadlock over Palestinian self-rule with increasing resistance and terrorism in the Israeli-occupied territories. Although the PLO and other groups over the years had continued to make sporadic attacks against Israel, violent confrontations now escalated. The new cycle of violence began in May 1980 with an incident in the West Bank town of Hebron in which Palestinian gunmen shot and killed six religious Jews. In response, Israel increased police patrols and deported three PLO leaders, spurring more violent attacks.

Palestinians became even more restless after Israel imposed a series of initiatives on them as the 1980s began. Israel believed that the PLO was preventing more moderate Palestinians from seeking peace, and so sought to curb the influence of the PLO on the Palestinian population. Israel thus decided to embark upon its own plan to establish a civilian government in the West Bank. In the fall of 1981 it appointed special Israeli civilian administrators, separating their function from Israel's military. In addition, Israel set up a new Palestinian political structure, which disbanded existing municipal councils and replaced them with a network of village leagues staffed by Arabs but appointed and funded by Israelis. This removed a group of Palestinian leaders with ties to the PLO and produced a system of local leaders more inclined to cooperate with Israeli authorities.

These actions to dominate Palestinian leadership incited more anger among the Palestinians, and led to increased Palestinian protests and violence. As American political scientist Mark Tessler describes, "With a scope and intensity unmatched during the previous fifteen years of Israeli occupation, the West Bank and Gaza exploded in the spring of 1982."[16]

Israel Invades Lebanon

Begin was reelected in 1981 and appointed a hard-line military general, Ariel Sharon, as Israel's defense minister. Sharon believed that the PLO was trying to turn Lebanon, as it had Jordan, into a base for striking at Israel. From its

The Entebbe Raid

During the late 1960s and the 1970s, in an effort to attract international attention to the Palestinian cause, Palestinian extremists conducted several airline hijackings. For example, on June 27, 1976, Palestinian terrorists hijacked an Air France passenger jet traveling from Israel to Paris. The hijackers released all non-Jewish passengers and flew the remaining Jewish passengers to Entebbe, Uganda. There, they were held hostage at the airport. The hijackers demanded that Israel release al-Fatah terrorists being held in Israeli jails.

A week passed while Israeli prime minister Yitzhak Rabin and his cabinet considered their options. Finally, on July 4 Israeli special forces, in a daring and successful airborne commando raid, made a five-thousand-mile round-trip flight to Uganda and rescued 103 trapped Jewish hostages. The terrorists were killed and only a few hostages died in the raid. In addition, one of the Israeli military men who took part in the raid was killed—Jonathan Netanyahu, the brother of Benjamin Netanyahu, who would later become prime minister of Israel. The Entebbe raid was viewed by Israelis as a great victory over terrorism.

positions on the Lebanese border with Israel, the PLO was shelling Israeli settlements, and the government of Lebanon was not acting to stop this development. In addition, Sharon was concerned about Syrian missiles located in Lebanon, which could be used to hit targets in Israel. On June 6, 1982, the Israeli army went into Lebanon with a huge force of over twenty thousand troops and 220 tanks. Later, Israeli forces increased to eighty thousand men and 1,240 tanks.

The Israeli invasion of Lebanon became very controversial. While Israel's professed goal was to clear the PLO from southern Lebanon and create a twenty-five-mile wide security zone on the Lebanese side of the border, Israeli defense minister Sharon carried out a much more aggressive campaign. Israeli forces advanced past the twenty-five-mile mark and attacked Beirut, Lebanon's capital city, killing thousands of Lebanese and Palestinian civilians, creating tens of thousands of refugees, and refusing to leave until the PLO was ousted from Lebanese territory. Along the way, Israel fought with Syrian ground and air forces,

Israeli soldiers fire at targets in Lebanon. In an effort to subdue the PLO presence there, Israel invaded the country in June 1982.

Mourners bear the coffin containing the body of pro-Israel Lebanese leader Bashir Gemayel. In 1982 Syrian agents sympathetic to the PLO assassinated Gemayel.

which were stationed in Lebanon, and destroyed Syria's missile system. By September 1982 PLO forces were forced out of Lebanon. Israel had begun to withdraw, and a multinational peacekeeping force was set up in Beirut.

However, the most controversial portion of the war occurred when pro-Israel Lebanese leader Bashir Gemayel was assassinated by Syrian agents who supported the PLO. After the assassination, Israeli troops reportedly permitted fol-

lowers of Bashir to enter Palestinian refugee camps to seek revenge, leading to a brutal massacre of between six and eight hundred Palestinian men, women, and children. The killings in the refugee camps (known as Sabra and Shatilla) were described as "butchery" by Israeli journalists Ze'ev Schiff and Ehud Ya'ari: "In addition to the wholesale slaughter of families, the [Bashir supporters] indulged in such sadistic horrors as hanging live grenades around their victims'

The Israeli Peace Movement

The peace protests in Israel after it invaded Lebanon were not the first time Israelis objected to government policies. Indeed, throughout Israel's history, a minority of its population has warned against the consequences of discriminating against the Arab population. As early as 1925 a peace group, called Brit Shalom, was formed; it urged that Palestine remain united and shared between Arabs and Jews, with each having equal rights. Later events in Israel's history, such as Israel's occupation of the West Bank and Gaza in the 1967 war, caused most Israelis who advocated peace to support dividing the land between Israel and the Palestinians, with varying ideas about how much land should be relinquished for a Palestinian state.

Peace Now activists demonstrate for peace in Israel.

Following Egyptian president Sadat's peace initiative in 1977, the Israeli government's decision to expand Israeli settlements in the West Bank and Gaza was viewed by some in Israel as a threat to peace. For example, as quoted by Andrew Rigby in his book, *Living the Intifada*, 350 reserve officers and soldiers at this time sent a letter to Israeli prime minister Begin warning that "a government policy that leads to the continued rule over one million Arabs is liable to damage the Jewish democratic character of the State. . . . True security will be achieved only with the advent of peace." The letter garnered widespread support for Peace Now, the most important and mainstream movement in the Israeli peace camp.

Peace Now organized numerous demonstrations protesting Israeli policies in the occupied territories. These efforts continued throughout Israel's war in Lebanon. Other peace groups also formed at this time, such as Pathways to Peace, a group of religious Zionists, and Yesh-Gvul, which was founded by a group of reserve soldiers at the start of the war in Lebanon. These soldiers published a letter stating their refusal to take part in Israel's action in Lebanon. By the end of the war, approximately 2,500 reserve soldiers signed the letter and about 160 were tried and sentenced for this action. Since then, Peace Now has continued its efforts along with other peace groups in Israel, but it has yet to win over the majority of Israelis.

necks. In one particularly vicious act of barbarity, an infant was trampled to death by a man wearing spiked shoes. The entire . . . action in Sabra and Shatilla seemed to be directed against civilians."[17]

The Sabra and Shatilla massacres brought worldwide condemnation of Israel and deeply shocked both Arabs and Israelis. In Israel, the massacres led to massive demonstrations against Israel's war in Lebanon. Many Israeli soldiers became conscientious objectors and refused to serve in Lebanon. For the Palestinians, the massacres fueled an already bub-bling caldron of rage against Israel and a sharp rise in tensions in the occupied territories. Israel finally left Beirut in May 1983 but maintained troops in southern Lebanon until 2000 to provide a security buffer.

In retrospect, the entire Lebanese campaign was a colossal failure for Israel. The war had cost Israel a million dollars a day, required it to rely on billions of dollars of U.S. aid to survive, and weakened Israel's economy. The PLO had been moved but not destroyed, and its leader, Yasir Arafat, had survived. In addition, the war had

Corpses litter a Beirut street after the 1982 Sabra and Shatilla massacres. The global community strongly condemned Israel's role in the massacres.

damaged Israelis' trust in their leaders, leading to the resignation of both Prime Minister Begin and Defense Minister Sharon, and to the election of a divided government in 1984 led by a new prime minister, Shimon Peres. Moreover, by inspiring Palestinians to increase their attacks on Israel, the war had served only to decrease Israel's security.

More Failed Peace Efforts

The years following Israel's withdrawal from Beirut saw the failure of several more attempts to revive peace negotiations amid ever-increasing Palestinian unrest. The first of these efforts came in September 1982, when U.S. president Ronald Reagan proposed a plan that called for a halt to further Jewish settle-

Prime Minister Manachem Begin (left) and Defense Minister Ariel Sharon resigned their posts following the 1982 Sabra and Shatilla massacres.

Hostages released after the hijacking of the cruise ship Achille Lauro *are taken ashore. The PLO-led attack was one of several that compromised Israeli/Palestinian relations in the mid-1980s.*

ments and a transition to eventual Palestinian self-government in the West Bank and Gaza areas. Reagan's plan was immediately rejected by Israel, and Arab leaders responded by proposing their own alternative peace plan.

At an Arab League summit in Fez, Morocco, the Arab states unanimously approved the Fez Plan, which recognized the PLO as the sole legitimate representative of the Palestinian people, recognized Israel in its pre-1967 borders, and called for Israeli withdrawal from all Arab territories seized in 1967. Israel, however, criticized the Fez proposal. The

Reagan administration, while praising it initially as a constructive step, immediately began to press Arab leaders to abandon the plan's inclusion of the PLO and its call for Palestinian independence. Ultimately, these discussions led both the PLO and Jordan to declare their opposition to the Reagan peace process, thereby ensuring its failure in the spring of 1983.

Yet another peace effort was made in 1983 by PLO leader Yasir Arafat, Egyptian president Hosni Mubarak, and Jordan's King Hussein. The three called for peace talks to be held at an international conference sponsored by the UN Security Council, with Palestinians represented by a joint Jordanian-Palestinian delegation. Their plan proposed Israeli withdrawal from the occupied territories, followed by direct talks between Jordan and the Palestinians to determine the fate of the territories. Although Israeli prime minister Shimon Peres refused to meet with PLO representatives, he agreed to begin direct peace negotiations with Jordan. Unfortunately, the talks never took place. Instead, relations between Israelis and Arabs deteriorated after a series of incidents. Among them were an Israeli attack on PLO headquarters in Tunisia; the shooting of several Israeli tourists by an Egyptian border guard; and the hijacking of an Italian cruise ship, the *Achille Lauro*, by PLO terrorists who murdered a Jewish passenger.

The final blow to the peace effort came when Arafat refused to sign a statement arranged by Jordan's King Hussein renouncing terrorism and recognizing Israel's right to exist. Although the PLO later agreed to sign the statement, Arafat killed the peace process by also insisting that the United States recognize the Palestinians' right to self-determination, a step America was not prepared to take. In February 1986 Jordan suspended its participation in the peace process and blamed the failure on the PLO.

The 1987 Intifada

What followed in 1987 was an intense uprising that became known as the first intifada, or resistance, by Palestinian civilians against the occupation and Israeli policies. Palestinian civilians had resisted Israel with periodic demonstrations and protests since its creation in 1948. The intifada, however, was a more desperate and violent form of protest, although still basically unarmed. As explained by sociologist Samih K. Farsoun, "Men, women, and children armed with the most readily available materials—stones, slingshots, burning debris, and makeshift barricades—[faced] one of the most advanced military forces in the world."[18] Indeed, one of the most tragic and enduring images of the intifada was that of Palestinian children throwing rocks at well-armed Israeli troops and tanks.

The spark that ignited the Palestinian uprising occurred on December 8, 1987, when an Israeli military vehicle plowed into a line of cars at a military checkpoint in Gaza, killing four Palestinians and injuring seven others. Afterward, although the crash was officially blamed on brake failure, a rumor spread among Palestinians that it was deliberate. News of the crash fanned the embers of an already smoldering Palestinian community.

After twenty years of repressive military rule by Israel, Palestinians were fed up with humiliating security checkpoints, arrests and deportation of political leaders, and brutal police crackdowns on all forms of protest. Palestinians were filled with resentment about confiscation of land to build a growing number of Israeli settlements and the failure of diplomatic efforts to improve the lives of Palestinians. Living in cramped, overcrowded ghettos, their hopes for jobs and schools strangled by Israel's oppressive policies, their dream of an independent state shattered, Palestinians had become desperate. As a result, over six thousand Palestinians spontaneously took to the streets in a massive and violent demonstration. Television images of the uprising were broadcast around the world.

Israeli troops, in an effort to disperse the crowds and restore law and order, responded harshly, with live ammunition, arrests, beatings, and tear gas. When the unrest continued, Israel instituted an "iron fist" policy that called for, among other tactics, using batons and rifle butts to break demonstrators' limbs, and raiding Palestinians' homes at night. During

A Palestinian (left) and an Israeli soldier clash during the first intifada, when Palestinian civilians protested violently against the Israeli occupation.

the first three months of the intifada, the Israeli army shot and killed more than one hundred Palestinian demonstrators, wounded hundreds more, and placed thousands under arrest and detention. Israel's response was criticized around the world, and notably by Jews in the United States.

The Israeli military crackdown only served to further galvanize the Palestinian community and escalate the familiar cycle of violence. Very quickly, the intifada spread to all sectors of Palestinian society, throughout the occupied territories and within Israel. As professor of sociology Samih K. Farsoun explains, "[The intifada] joined together the young and the old, men and women, urban dwellers and villagers, Muslims and Christians, the poor and the rich, and all political currents to form a genuine grassroots movement."[19]

In addition, the PLO organized economic attacks on the Israeli economy,

A hooded Palestinian holds up a Palestinian flag during a series of riots during which demonstrators lashed out against Israel's repressive military rule.

such as boycotts of Israeli products and tax revolts. Israel responded to the growing revolt with improved military riot control tactics, economic punishments, detention and imprisonment of thousands, and strict and prolonged curfews that confined Palestinians to their homes.

The demonstrations, boycotts, and general unrest continued through 1993 and cost much suffering and many lives. By the end of the fighting, 1,087 Palestinian civilians had been killed by Israel forces and 143 Israelis, both civilians and soldiers, were killed by Palestinians. Thousands more were injured on both sides. In addition, 1,473 Palestinian houses were demolished.

The intifada, however, marked a turning point in Israeli-Palestinian relations. This was the first popular uprising of the Palestinian people against Israel. For the first time, ordinary Palestinians did not rely on other Arab nations or even their own militant leaders to negotiate with or strike at Israel; instead, they themselves faced down their Israeli oppressors, showing their determination not to be oppressed, marginalized, or eliminated. The intifada failed to bring an end to Israeli occupation in the West Bank and Gaza Strip, but it showed that ordinary Palestinians would not submit to Israeli policies. Indeed, the fierceness of the uprising shocked Israelis and renewed criticism of the nation's policies in the occupied territories. Other Israelis, however, reacted by favoring even more hard-line policies against the Palestinians. In any case, the intifada won international support for the Palestinian cause, leading many on both sides to the conclusion that a political solution was now desperately needed to resolve the Arab-Israeli conflict.

CHAPTER 4

Turning Toward Peace

The parties involved in the Arab-Israeli conflict reacted to the 1987 intifada by concentrating their efforts toward finding a peaceful solution. Jordan, like Egypt, bowed out of the conflict and made its own peace with Israel. The PLO officially renounced terrorism and violence and agreed to recognize Israel's right to exist. Israel, in turn, finally agreed to negotiate directly with the PLO. The result of these shifts was a historic agreement between Israel and the Palestinians that paved the way for a future, permanent Middle East peace. These efforts came very close to resolving the Arab-Israeli conflict, but not close enough.

Arafat Makes Concessions

The first change produced by the intifada was an announcement by King Hussein of Jordan. Frustrated by the lack of progress in past talks and by the PLO chairman Arafat's stubborn positions, Jordan abandoned its administration of the West Bank and revoked the Jordanian citizenship of Palestinians living there. This action eliminated the option of having Jordan represent the Palestinians in peace negotiations, an idea often favored by the United States and Israel. It also reaffirmed the PLO's status as the only logical representative for the Palestinian people.

Arafat decided to take advantage of this new opportunity. At a November 1988 meeting, the PLO declared the independence of Palestine. Just as important, Arafat called for a resolution to the conflict based on UN Resolutions 242 and 338, implicitly accepting that Israel must be recognized as a legitimate nation and that the Palestinians would accept land in the occupied territories in exchange for peace. Arafat followed this action with a speech and press conference at a meeting of the UN General Assembly in Geneva in December 1988, where he renounced terrorism and articulated the PLO's recognition of Israel. These statements were dramatic; the PLO recognized Israel's right to exist for the first time in its history, a major step for a group that had previously been dedicated to Israel's destruction. Arafat's statements raised hopes among many Palestinians that the parties could now directly negotiate an end to the violence and a permanent peace treaty.

However, for some extremist Palestinians, Arafat's statements were too much of a sacrifice. They felt he had betrayed the historic Palestinian position that Israel had no right to exist on any

Yasir Arafat speaks before the UN General Assembly in 1988. During the speech, Arafat renounced terrorism and recognized Israel's right to exist.

lands that had previously been home to Arabs. According to this view, all of Palestine rightly belonged to the Palestinians, including not only the territories but also all of Israel itself. The terrorist group Hamas, for example, stated: "We condemn all the attitudes calling for ending the *jihad* [holy war] and struggle, and for establishing peace with the murderers, and the attitudes which call for acceptance of the Jewish entity on any part of our land."[20] The new PLO position, therefore, divided Palestinians, some of whom celebrated the PLO move as a practical choice for peace, and others who favored the more radical positions of terrorist groups such as Hamas and the Islamic Jihad.

In addition, Israel's response was disappointing. Instead of making a similarly bold move that could advance peace prospects, Israel's Prime Minister Yitzhak Shamir continued to refuse to negotiate with the PLO; he and many others in Israel considered the PLO to be a terrorist organization that must be destroyed. Israel offered a new peace proposal, but it soon faltered over the question of who would speak for the Palestinians.

The Effect of the Gulf War on Peace Efforts

In 1990 the Arab-Israeli conflict was eclipsed by Iraq's invasion of Kuwait and the ensuing U.S.-led Persian Gulf War; nevertheless, the war had an important impact on Israeli-Palestinian relations. Even before the war began, Iraq had embraced the Palestinian cause by providing pensions to families of Palestinians who were killed in the intifada. In addition, Iraqi president Saddam Hussein threatened to attack Israel with chemical weapons; such an attack, Saddam be-

Arafat Renounces Terrorism and Recognizes Israel

On December 14, 1988, Palestine Liberation Organization (PLO) leader Yasir Arafat explicitly recognized Israel's right to exist, a reversal of previous PLO policy which insisted that Israel must be destroyed and all of Palestine returned to the Palestinians. Also for the first time, Arafat renounced terrorism, which the PLO had used since its inception. In a speech reprinted in A Concise History of the Arab-Israeli Conflict *Arafat said:*

Self-determination means survival for the Palestinians and our survival does not destroy the survival of the Israelis as their rulers claim. . . . [W]e mean our people's freedom and national independence . . . and the right of all parties concerned in the Middle East conflict to exist in peace and security . . . including the state of Palestine, Israel and other neighbors. . . . As for terrorism, . . . I repeat for the record that we totally and absolutely renounce all forms of terrorism, including individual, group and state terrorism. . . . Enough is enough. Enough is enough. Enough is enough.

An Israeli neighborhood lies in ruins after a SCUD missile attack. During the 1990 Gulf War, Iraqi leader Saddam Hussein fired thirty-nine SCUD missiles at Israel.

lieved, could break up the international coalition that was forming to fight him, or at least weaken support from Arab members of the coalition such as Saudi Arabia, Egypt, and Syria. During the war, in an attempt to broaden the conflict into an Arab-Israeli conflict, Saddam offered to withdraw from Kuwait if the Israelis left the occupied territories. He also tried dragging Israel into the war, firing thirty-nine SCUD missiles at Israel, causing two deaths, hundreds of injuries, and extensive property damage.

Israel, however, agreed to a U.S. request not to respond to the Iraqi strikes, a difficult choice for a nation committed to taking strong military action in response to Arab attacks. Israel made this choice because its participation in the war might have weakened or disrupted the anti-Iraq coalition and jeopardized the victory that the United States and other countries hoped to achieve. This overall victory—the elimination of the Iraqi threat—was what was most important for Israel's long-term security. With the Iraqi enemy neutralized, international support high because of its restraint policy, and its citizens united, Israel emerged from the war in a much stronger position.

Conversely, the war weakened support for Arafat and the PLO. Although every Arab state except Libya condemned Iraq's action, Arafat made a fateful decision to back Saddam Hussein. Arafat had several loyalties to Iraq; not only had Saddam long championed the Palestinian cause, but Iraq had also financially supported Palestinians in the intifada. Arafat may have believed Saddam would win the Gulf War or at least do serious damage to Israel, but the strategy backfired; Arafat's position severely damaged his credibility with the United States and Israel and resulted in only more pain for Palestinians. After the war, Israel took actions such as dramatically cutting the number of Palestinians permitted to work in Israel. The Arab states reduced their charitable contributions to the Palestinian cause. With Iraq's defeat, the Palestinians were isolated and once again disgraced.

The Madrid Peace Conference

Flush with its victory over Iraq, the United States tried to use the momentum to push for an international peace conference to resolve the Arab-Israeli issues. At the urging of U.S. president George H.W. Bush and with Soviet sponsorship, an international peace conference convened on October 20, 1991, in Madrid, Spain. Representatives to the conference included Israel, Syria, Lebanon, and Jordan. However, because Israel still refused to meet with the PLO, only non-PLO Palestinians were permitted to attend the conference, and they attended as part of the Jordan delegation in the status of observers and advisers rather than participants.

The Madrid conference, as journalists Ahron Bregman and Jihan el-Tahri explain, was hailed as "the biggest breakthrough in Arab-Israeli relations since President Sadat's historic visit to Israel . . . [because] Israeli and Arab leaders sat down at the same table to begin negotiations."[21] The conference sought to create a comprehensive Middle East peace with two levels of negotiation: (1) multilateral talks between Israel and the Arab states about key Middle East problems; and (2) bilateral talks in which Israel would talk directly with each Arab state, including a joint Jordanian-Palestinian delegation, about the Israeli-Palestinian conflict.

Unfortunately, little progress was made at Madrid or in subsequent negotiations. After the more moderate Labor Party won elections in Israel in 1992 based on a peace platform, new Labor prime minister Yitzhak Rabin took actions designed to help the peace process, such as freeing more than eight hundred Palestinian prisoners and stopping private sector building in the occupied territories. However, the Palestinian delegation, completely controlled by the PLO, firmly insisted on more substantive goals, such as the creation of a Palestinian self-governing authority and eventually an independent Palestinian state.

The lack of progress in the talks took its toll on Palestinians. The intifada continued, Arafat's leadership began to be questioned, and radical Palestinian groups such as Hamas and others gained more support, posing a growing threat to the PLO. In addition, the PLO was losing support because of financial problems; due largely to a drastic cutback in funding from Arab states as a result of Arafat's support for Saddam Hussein, the PLO was forced to reduce its assistance

Arab Treatment of the Palestinians

Although the Palestinians blame their plight largely on Israel, they also have been betrayed and mistreated by neighboring Arab states. At the end of the 1948 war against Israel, for example, the Palestinians could have established an independent state in the parts of Palestine that Israel did not occupy. However, both Jordan and Egypt invaded and occupied the non-Israeli portions of East Palestine and Gaza from 1948 until 1967, when Israel gained control of these territories. In addition, some Arab states treated the Palestinian refugees badly. Only Jordan granted Palestinians full citizenship and provided opportunities for work and advancement; in Syria and Lebanon, citizenship was not offered and many Palestinians continued to live in poverty in refugee camps.

In truth, Palestinians have mostly received only verbal support from the Arab countries, not meaningful backing. In 1970, for example, King Hussein of Jordan booted the PLO out of his country, forcing it to relocate its headquarters in Lebanon, where Israeli attacks in 1982 caused yet another move to Tunis. In 1973 the Arab-Israeli war gave Arab countries an excuse to raise oil prices, but they did not use the oil weapon to gain concessions for the Palestinians. Later, although both Egypt and Jordan, the leading Arab states, claimed to represent the interests of the Palestinians in peace negotiations with Israel, both failed to secure deals to provide for Palestinian independence and instead opted for separate peace deals with Israel. Sadat's Camp David Accords, for example, secured peace with Israel for Egypt at the expense of Palestinian independence. Similarly, after Oslo, Jordan made peace with Israel, abandoning the Palestinians' dream for independence. Today, most Arab states continue to express support for Palestinian independence, but only states such as Syria and Lebanon provide concrete support, in the form of funding and training for Palestinian terrorist groups.

to Palestinians in the occupied territories just when they needed it most.

Finally, in December 1992, the bilateral Palestinian-Israeli talks abruptly ended when Hamas kidnapped an Israeli border policeman, Nissim Toledano, demanding that Israel release Hamas leader Sheikh Ahmed Yassin from jail. Israel responded by deporting 415 Hamas members to Lebanon, creating an international crisis when Lebanon refused to accept them. Israel's multilateral talks with Lebanon, Syria, and Jordan also stalled after the incident.

The Oslo Peace Agreements

Despite the setbacks, the peace process was revived by secret talks between the PLO and Israel in Oslo, Norway, in 1993, producing two historic agreements that moved the two sides closer than ever to a permanent peace. The secret

President Bill Clinton looks on as Israeli prime minister Yitzhak Rabin (left) and PLO leader Yasir Arafat accept the Oslo I Agreement in September 1993.

meetings began as an informal and unofficial attempt to revive formal stalled peace talks. They were approved by both Arafat and Rabin. The meetings went on for seven months and produced an Israeli-Palestinian agreement on August 20, 1993, that formed the basis for a dramatic interim peace deal between Israel and the PLO.

The agreement provided for Palestinian self-rule in parts of the occupied territories and for elections to create a Palestinian government, called the Palestinian Authority, to govern the areas. Negotiations on permanent peace issues, such as Palestinian independence, Israeli withdrawal from settlements, and the status of Jerusalem were postponed until later. What became known as the Oslo I Agreement was signed on September 13, 1993, at a remarkable ceremony held at the White House in Washington, D.C., and presided over by U.S. president Bill Clinton. After the signing, the world witnessed an amazing sight—a handshake between two sworn enemies, PLO chairman Arafat and Israeli prime minister Rabin.

The Oslo Agreement was a major step in the Arab-Israeli peace process. It marked the very first time the Palestinians and Israel had held direct peace negotiations with each other. As historian Martin Gilbert describes: "[The Arafat-Rabin] handshake, as much as any other single act, symbolized the revolution and the new reality: Israel had recognized the PLO, was talking to it, and was signing agreements with it, and the PLO had recognized Israel."[22] Indeed, on December 10, 1994, Arafat, Rabin, and Israeli foreign minister Shimon Peres received the Nobel Peace Prize for their roles in the peace process.

Oslo I was followed in 1995 by the Oslo II Agreement, which dealt with the details of how to transfer control over the occupied territories to the Palestinians. Under the terms of Oslo II, the Palestinian Authority was given legislative, executive, and judicial powers, as well as full control over security, education, health, and welfare of the Palestinians. The agreement also provided for elections; these were held on January 20, 1996, and Arafat won, becoming president of the Palestinian Authority.

However, the substance of the Oslo agreements left much to be desired for the Palestinians. Indeed, because the agreements dealt only with limited Palestinian self-rule, and not sovereignty over the land, many Palestinians saw them as a sellout by Arafat of the Palestinian cause. By conceding so much and postponing talks about the issues most important to Palestinians—independence and removal of Israeli settlements, the establishment of Jerusalem as the Palestinian capital, and the right of return for refugees of the 1948 War of Independence—Arafat was seen as sacrificing decades of Palestinian suffering for nothing. Walid Khalidi, a Palestinian professor at Harvard, for example, described Oslo as "a Zionist composition in terminology, purpose and detail,"[23] because it benefitted the Israelis so much. Nevertheless, Khalidi and other Palestinians hoped that the Oslo deal would be the starting point for a process that could someday lead to a sovereign Palestinian state.

The main result of the two Oslo agreements was that Israel quickly pulled its troops out of some of the occupied areas in Gaza and Jericho (a small district in the West Bank), and later from some of the major Palestinian cities. Most of the occupied territories in Gaza and the West Bank remained under Israeli occupation and control, with the West Bank divided into three zones. Under the terms of Oslo II, in the first zone of six Palestinian cities, Israeli troops were to be withdrawn to the suburbs; in the second zone encompassing about 450 towns in rural areas, the Israeli military and Palestinian police were to share authority and conduct joint patrols; finally, in the third zone, covering existing and future Israeli settlements and military installations, Israel retained full control.

In the end, therefore, Israel withdrew from only about 30 percent of the West Bank. As sociologist Samih K. Farsoun put it, the Palestinian Authority "gained limited civil authority over less than 4 percent of the area of historic Palestine,"[24] while the agreements allowed Israel to keep its 1948 borders as well as most of the lands it occupied in 1967, where Israel continued to build more settlements.

A Jordanian-Israeli Peace, Palestinian Despair and Violence

In the post-Oslo period, Jordan's King Hussein moved to end hostilities between Jordan and Israel. On October 26, 1994, Hussein and Rabin signed a formal peace treaty. Israel now had peace with two of its most important Arab neighbors—

Egypt and Jordan. The Jordan-Israel negotiations prompted other Arab countries to change their policies toward Israel. For example, Morocco and Tunisia each established limited diplomatic contacts with the Jewish state.

The Jordanian-Israeli peace deal, like the Egyptian-Israeli peace agreement, indicated that the Arab world had abandoned the Palestinian cause. The Arab states were willing to make peace and accept the existence of Israel, giving Israel what it wanted without first achieving an independent Palestinian state. This realization left Palestinians feeling impotent and full of rage because their condition was not improving. As one resident of the West Bank described, "[After Oslo] we believed we would have safe land, a good economy, and unquestioned dignity, and our own state . . . [but the] situation is worse since Oslo. Mix the truth of our lives with the hopes of our lives and you get an emotion that smells to me like gunpowder, which, as you know, can explode."[25]

As a result, the Jordanian-Israeli peace process, together with the Oslo peace accords, produced an upsurge of terrorism and violence in the Middle East by Palestinians opposed to the agreements. For example, a new terrorist group began taking up the Palestinian cause—an Iranian-backed Islamic group called Hizballah, based in Lebanon. In addition, both Hamas and the Islamic Jihad increased their attacks on Israel, using a relatively new tactic—suicide bombers who blew themselves up in Israel along with innocent Israeli civilians. As Israeli sociologist Baruch Kimmerling describes, "Being pre-

An Israeli police jeep leaves the Palestinian town of Ramallah in December 1995, relinquishing control of the area to the PLO in accord with the Oslo agreements.

cisely guided human missiles, suicide bombers caused heavy, mainly civilian, casualties among the Israelis, paralyzed daily life almost completely, and badly damaged Israeli morale."[26] Among Pales-

tinians, the suicide bombers are honored as martyrs who make the supreme sacrifice for the Palestinian cause.

For Israelis, however, they were terrorists and murderers of innocent men,

Palestinians pass through an Israeli checkpoint. The Israeli government set up similar checkpoints throughout the country as a security measure against Palestinian terrorism.

women, and children. Israel's response was to take security actions, such as increasing road checkpoints and closing its borders to tens of thousands of Palestinians. This prevented Palestinian workers from traveling to their jobs and stopped goods from being transported into and out of the territories. It also led to a sharp rise in unemployment and reduced exports and investments, which made Palestinian lives even more difficult. As tensions escalated between Israelis and Palestinians, popular support for compromise and negotiation diminished on both sides.

The Oslo Peace Process Falters

As a result of increasing Palestinian terrorism, extreme opposition to Rabin's peace negotiations increased in Israel. Indeed, fanatics on both sides—Palestinian terrorists who insisted the land was for Arabs only, and ultrareligious Jews who insisted God had given the land to the Jewish people—were unwilling to make peace under any circumstances.

Jewish student Yigal Amir heads into court after confessing to the assassination of Israeli prime minister Yitzhak Rabin in 1995.

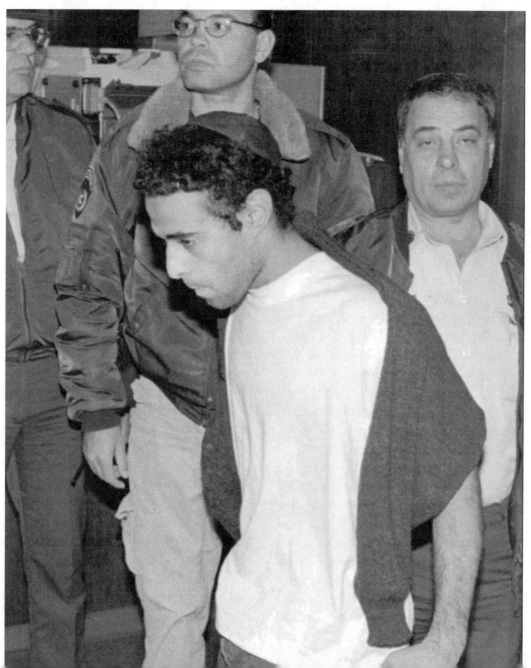

One such extremist took irrevocable action that resulted in tragedy and placed peace negotiations further in doubt. On November 4, 1995, Yigal Amir, a Jewish student, assassinated Israeli prime minister Yitzhak Rabin in Tel Aviv, where Rabin had addressed a peace rally attended by over one hundred thousand Israelis. His murder shocked the entire world, especially when it was discovered that the killer was a Jew. Amir said he was acting on God's orders to prevent Israel from being given to the Palestinians. Ironically, just before he died, Rabin had declared: "[The peace process] is a course which is fraught with difficulties and pain. . . . But the path of peace is preferable to the path of war. . . . [F]or our children . . . I want this government to exhaust every opening, every possibility, to promote and achieve a comprehensive peace."[27] The incident made clear the wide differences in Israeli opinion about Israel's peace efforts and severely strained the peace process.

Indeed, the peace that Rabin was seeking seemed to die with him. His successor, Prime Minister Benjamin Netanyahu, was not as open to negotiations and peacemaking, as evidenced by his election slogan, "Peace with Security."[28] Netanyahu, claiming there could be no peace before Israelis had security, stalled on some of Israel's promises made during Oslo. He delayed Israel's withdrawal from some areas designated as Palestinian areas in Oslo II and built new Israeli settlements in the West Bank. In a move that perhaps best illustrated his hard-line, aggressive approach to the peace process, he selected former defense minister Ariel Sharon, the leader of Israel's 1982 war on Lebanon, to serve in his cabinet. Also, shortly after his election, Netanyahu ordered the opening of an archaeological tunnel in Jerusalem under what is known to Jews as the Temple Mount and to Muslims as al-Aqsa Mosque, one of Judaism's and Islam's holiest sites. This caused a riot among Palestinians, who feared Israel was endangering the holy location. Thereafter, Israel's negotiating relationship with the Palestinians quickly deteriorated.

Nevertheless, Netanyahu reluctantly continued the Oslo peace process. He and Arafat were able to negotiate an agreement in 1997 providing for Israel to withdraw from Hebron, an area covered by the Oslo accords that Netanyahu had resisted leaving. Also, with U.S. president Bill Clinton acting as mediator, the parties in October 1998 signed an agreement called the Wye Memorandum that renewed the Oslo process, turned over more land to Palestinian control, and paved the way for talks about the final status of peace between Israel and the Palestinians. Indeed, as a result of these peace agreements, many of Netanyahu's more conservative supporters deserted him, bringing about his political downfall.

Camp David Hopes and the Collapse of the Peace Process

Netanyahu's defeat brought new Israeli leaders into the government, leading Israel and the Palestinians to peace talks that came very, very close to resolving

Barak's Speech After Camp David

After Israeli prime minister Ehud Barak returned to Israel from the failed 2000 Camp David peace talks on July 26, 2000, he gave a speech describing his disappointment over the failure of the peace talks (reprinted from the Israel Ministry of Foreign Affairs Web site):

> Fifteen days ago, I set out from Jerusalem, the heart of the Jewish people, on a mission of peace in Camp David. In the name of millions of citizens raising their eyes in hope and in prayer, I embarked to try and complete the task begun by the late Menachem Begin, and for which the late Yitzhak Rabin gave his life. In your name, I set out to bring peace and hope to our children and to put an end to the 100-year-old conflict between us and our Palestinian neighbors. . . . Today I return from Camp David, and can look into the millions of eyes and say with regret: We have not yet succeeded. We did not succeed because we did not find a partner prepared to make decisions on all issues. We did not succeed because our Palestinian neighbors have not yet internalized the fact that in order to achieve peace, each side has to give up some of their dreams; to give, not only to demand. I look into the millions of eyes in whose name we embarked on this mission, and say: We did everything we could.

the Arab-Israeli conflict. In May 1999 Labor Party candidate Ehud Barak was elected as Israel's prime minister as part of a campaign that promised to continue Rabin's peace efforts. Barak reopened peace talks with the Palestinians in 1999 to address the issues necessary for a permanent peace between the two sides.

The talks resulted in another Camp David, Maryland, summit meeting in July 2000—this time between U.S. president Bill Clinton, Palestinian Authority president Yasir Arafat, and new Israeli prime minister Ehud Barak. The negotiations, guided by Clinton, were very difficult but remarkably led to what many regarded as a very generous and courageous offer by Barak. Although

never publicly released, the proposal reportedly provided for much of what the Palestinians had been seeking—an independent Palestinian state in the West Bank and Gaza and the removal of a large number of Jewish settlements. For those settlements that would remain in Palestinian areas, the agreement provided for the Palestinians to be compensated with other Israeli land. In addition, Palestinians were given control over East Jerusalem and religious sovereignty over the Temple Mount.

However, the peace process at Camp David collapsed when Arafat rejected Israel's offer without even offering a counterproposal. Arafat's rejection has been explained as a reluctance to share

Jerusalem, which Palestinians sought as the capital of Palestine in its entirety, and not securing a right of return for the hundreds of thousands of Palestinian refugees. Clinton, however, placed the blame for failure of the talks squarely on Arafat, concluding that he had just given up the best peace deal ever offered to the Palestinians. When Arafat called Clinton three days before Clinton left office to say good-bye, Arafat told him he was a "great man"; Clinton responded, "The hell I am, I'm a colossal failure, and you made me one."[29]

The Camp David talks were the closest the Palestinians and the Israelis had ever gotten to resolving their differences and ending the ongoing violence. Their failure plunged the two sides into yet another round of violence.

CHAPTER 5

The Conflict Continues

The most recent phase of the Arab-Israeli conflict began with yet another Palestinian uprising, sparked by the actions of Ariel Sharon, a leader of the Israeli Likud Party known for his hard-line political views. This second Palestinian intifada was even more violent than the first Palestinian resistance movement in 1987. It led to an unprecedented military assault by Israel against Palestinians as well as to a decline of U.S. support for Arafat as a partner for peace.

The Second Intifada

The collapse of the 2000 Camp David peace talks raised the already high frustrations of Palestinians to a new level. Not only had Palestinians lived with Israeli oppression and military occupation for decades and been abandoned by other Arab nations; now, after a long and patient peace process, Arafat's rejection of the peace plan left the Palestinians with nothing.

Frustration turned to violence after September 28, 2000, when Ariel Sharon, in a provocative and ill-timed move, visited the Temple Mount in Jerusalem accompanied by about fifteen hundred Israeli policemen. The Temple Mount site, which contains al-Aqsa mosque and the western wall of the ancient Jewish temple, is sacred to both Jews and Muslims. Due to Sharon's history of conducting excessive military actions against the Palestinians, his presence at the holy site triggered stone throwing and protests by Palestinians. The demonstrations quickly grew into a violent grassroots protest. As in the first intifada, pent up frustrations and rage exploded from Palestinian civilians as well as from Palestinian militia groups. This revolt

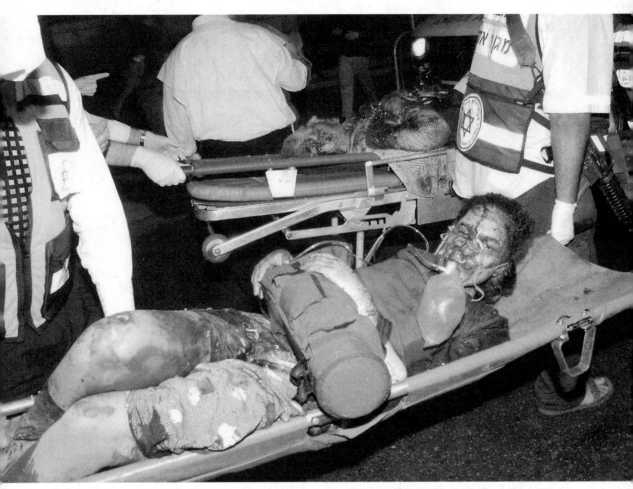

Medics evacuate two badly wounded Israeli victims of a suicide bombing. During the second intifada, Palestinian terrorists launched a wave of suicide bombers.

would become known among Palestinians as the al-Aqsa intifada, after al-Aqsa mosque.

In the first intifada, rock-throwing Palestinian children and Palestinian police officers with small weapons were pitted against Israeli riot police armed with tear gas, guns, tanks, and helicopter gunships. The second intifada, however, quickly became a fully armed revolt, as both civilians and members of Palestinian militia groups joined the protest with bombs and firearms, which they used to target Israeli settlers as well as Israeli soldiers. The second intifada also launched a wave of Palestinian suicide bombers who attacked civilians within Israel's borders. Indeed, the suicide bomber became the strongest symbol of the al-Aqsa intifada.

Suicide Bombers

The suicide bombers are weapons used mainly by three extreme Islamic Palestinian groups: Hamas, Islamic Jihad, and a new group, the Al-Aqsa Martyrs

Brigades. These groups believe that suicide bombing is the most effective tactic that underfunded, under-armed Palestinians can use against the enormous power and might of the Israeli military. With this tactic, the Palestinian extremists provoke fear among Israelis, which they hope will lead to Israel's complete withdrawal from the occupied territories and to an independent Palestinian nation. Suicide attacks are carefully planned, similar to military operations, and are timed to get the most media coverage. Suicide bombers typically board a bus, enter a busy restaurant or a crowded shop, and blow themselves up using explosives with a hand-pulled detonator. They try to maximize damage to structures and civilians by choosing places that are busy places of business.

Suicide bombers tend to be unmarried Islamic men in their late teens or early twenties. They believe that their actions will allow them to go straight to paradise, where they will be honored by God. Bombers are recruited by militants at mosques and religious schools. After the bombings, Palestinian militant and charitable groups typically provide for the bombers' families. The bombers are usually honored as martyrs for the Palestinian cause.

During the first three years of the second intifada, the Palestinians made more than one hundred suicide and bomb attacks on Israel. In one of the deadliest suicide bomb attacks, a Hamas suicide bomber in March 2002 blew himself up in a hotel in the Israeli resort of Netanya, killing twenty-eight Israelis who were celebrating the Jewish holiday of Passover.

The suicide tactics, however, did not entice Israel into negotiating a Palestinian state; on the contrary, Israel's position

A Suicide Bombing

On a Saturday night in December 2001, twins Eran and Avi Mizrahi were celebrating their sixteenth birthday with their friends at a café in central Jerusalem. As Eran and Avi began opening their birthday gifts, two Palestinian suicide bombers entered the café and blew themselves up.

Both teenagers were injured, but Eran was almost killed. He was hit with a screw from the suicide bomb that lodged in the front lobe of his brain. After the bomb attack, Eran had no pulse and was not breathing; he was rushed into surgery. After surgery, Eran could no longer speak and could only write a few words. Avi suffered only minor physical injuries, but he remembers the white smoke from the blast and seeing his brother's body lying on the pavement.

As quoted by news correspondent Megan Goldin in a piece called "An Israeli Family's Story," contained in a book by Reuters, *The Israeli-Palestinian Conflict: Crisis in the Middle East*, Avi's and Eran's father, Rafi Mizrahi, said his Arab friends have expressed their sympathy and he does not blame the Palestinians: "I pity the Palestinian nation. They don't want this." Instead, Rafi said he blames Yasir Arafat and Israeli leaders for what happened to his children.

was hardened and it used its military might to retaliate. The suicide bombings also destroyed much of the world's sympathy for the plight of the Palestinians; whereas many nations did not condone the Israeli occupation, they certainly did not condone the use of terrorism to achieve political goals.

Israel Cracks Down on the Palestinian Revolt

Israel responded to the intifada violence with overwhelming military force. In addition to sending out troops, Israel implemented a policy of targeted assassinations of Palestinian leaders believed to be responsible for terrorist acts. The

The Israeli government responded to the second intifada with tremendous military force. Soldiers like these were sent into the occupied territories in search of terrorist leaders.

assassinations often resulted in the killing of innocent persons along with the target of the raids.

Israel might drop a missile on a suspected Palestinian leader's house, killing him but also killing innocent people in the surrounding area, along with damaging much property.

Despite UN condemnation of Israel's excessive use of force and calls for an end to the violence, the death toll mounted on both sides. In the wake of this violence, on February 6, 2001, Israeli voters fed up with the fighting opted to elect Ariel Sharon as their new prime minister. He won by a landslide. His election ensured that Israel's policies would become even more hard-line.

In March 2002 Sharon implemented Operation Defensive Shield, a plan designed to wipe out the Palestinian terror network. As part of this plan, Israeli tanks and troops supported by Apache helicopters were sent to the West Bank and Gaza. The Israeli forces tried to disarm the entire population and remove caches of arms and explosives. They also arrested thousands of Palestinians accused of supporting terrorism; between February 27 and May 20, 2002, Amnesty International (an international peace organization) estimated that approximately eighty-five hundred persons were arrested and interrogated.

"They Create a Desolation and Call It Peace"

In addition, the Israelis systematically damaged or completely destroyed civilian Palestinian targets. On the pretext of finding terrorists, Israeli troops bulldozed the homes of known Palestinian suicide bombers, punishing entire families for the actions of one individual family member. Indeed, more than four thousand homes were demolished by Israeli troops in the operation.

The Israeli Defense Force troops also demolished schools, clinics, and mosques, as well as Palestinian infrastructure, such as water treatment facilities, power plants, and roads. The environment was similarly destroyed; about 170,000 Palestinian trees that had taken decades to reach maturity were uprooted. The operation devastated an already beleaguered Palestinian economy and made everyday life for many Palestinians extremely difficult. Indeed, Israeli philosophy professor Haim Gordon says of Israel's operation, "They create a desolation and call it peace."[30]

Most Palestinians offered little to no resistance, but in the refugee camp at Jenin there was fierce fighting. After the Netanya Passover suicide bombing, the IDF was sent to Jenin to root out suspected terrorists there. Various Palestinian groups such as Hamas, al-Fatah, and Islamic Jihad, however, had booby-trapped the camp before Israeli troops arrived, leading them into a trap.

For three days, the Israelis were held off, until they brought in bulldozers and passed from house to house by knocking down walls. Rumors of a massacre circulated, and Israel refused to allow UN observers, the media, or rescue teams into the area. Palestinians claimed that hundreds of people were killed, but Israel said the death toll was much lower and disputed the accusation of a massacre. Israel did admit that it had used excessive force in Jenin, including actions considered to be war crimes, such as using human shields, taking hostages, and denying aid to the injured.

Many, including members of the Israeli government, condemned Israel's harsh actions in Jenin and elsewhere. For example, Ephrayim Sneh, then Israel's minister of education, was quoted on April 20, 2002, in an Israeli newspaper criticizing Sharon as a war criminal: "Sharon will appear at the International Criminal Court at The Hague—without me."[31]

On April 21, 2002, Israel officially declared Operation Defensive Shield over, but Israeli troops nevertheless continued to enter Palestinian areas to make arrests. At the same time, Palestinians continued their suicide attacks on Israel. In June 2002 Israel launched another military operation, called Operation Determined Path, reoccupying many Palestinian areas.

The High Cost of the Intifada

By the fall of 2002 the intifada had resulted in the death of thousands of people, many of them children. Indeed, in October 2002 Amnesty International condemned both Israel and the Palestinians for their "utter disregard"[32] for the lives of children. The group's report estimated that 250 Palestinian and 72 Israeli children had been killed in the conflict. In addition, forty-five hundred Israelis and about twenty thousand Palestinians had been injured in the fighting.

For the Palestinians, however, the conflict had costs in addition to the horrible loss of life. Previous Israeli security actions,

such as the curfews and closures on the occupied territories after the Oslo accords, had hurt the Palestinian economy, but as noted by professor Efraim Karsh, "By the beginning of 1999 . . . the West Bank and Gaza had fully recovered from the economic decline of the previous years."[33] The second intifada and Israel's forceful response, however, delivered a devastating blow to the Palestinian economy. The United Nations estimated that the Israeli raids stopped much of Palestinian business production and idled as many as three-quarters of the Palestinian people. Homes, schools, businesses, banks, government offices, and roads were simply gone. This time, only massive humanitarian and reconstruction efforts could repair the damage. Indeed, even as the fighting continued, the International Red Cross warned of serious food, water, and medicine shortages, and the United Nations began distributing food; by midsummer 2003 international agencies were feeding about 1.8 million Palestinians.

The intifada also brought a complete end to peace talks, which had continued in a fragile state after Camp David 2000. Sharon, however, refused to talk while the intifada continued, and Arafat either would not or could not stop the violence. Also, in January 2001 U.S. president Clinton left office and a more conservative American president, George W. Bush, took his place. Negotiators for Israel and the Palestinians met at the Egyptian resort of Taba between January 22 and January 28, 2001, and although Israel reportedly made even further concessions at those talks, no agreement could be reached while the intifada continued.

Arafat's Confinement in Ramallah

At the start of the second intifada, Israel sought to isolate PLO leader and Palestinian Authority president Yasir Arafat because it held him responsible for terrorism against Israel. In September 2002, in response to a suicide bomb attack on Israel, Israeli troops surrounded Arafat's West Bank headquarters in the city of Ramallah and placed him under house arrest. In addition, using tanks and bulldozers, Israel virtually demolished the PLO compound. The extent of the damage was extensive. Although once a sprawling compound the size of a city block, the PLO headquarters was reduced to one three-story building that housed Arafat's offices and living areas, guard facilities, and offices and sleeping quarters for aides. Israeli attacks then destroyed much of this building, including Arafat's first-floor office, dining room, and bedroom, and stairs leading to the third floor, confining Arafat to four rooms in one wing on the second floor.

Thereafter, the Israelis prohibited Arafat from leaving the compound until he handed over colleagues wanted by Israel for terrorist activities. Eventually, as a result of American intervention, and after Arafat turned over the men sought by Israel, the Israelis said Arafat would be permitted to leave. However, because the Israelis would not guarantee that he would be allowed back into Ramallah if he left, Arafat remained isolated, living and working in his bombed-out headquarters there. Israel's unprecedented action was condemned by many but it ultimately succeeded in weakening Arafat in the eyes of many frustrated Palestinians.

In 2002, in response to a suicide attack in Israel, the Israeli military surrounded and bombarded Yasir Arafat's PLO compound.

Similarly, a peace proposal from Saudi crown prince Abdullah went nowhere. Under these conditions, prospects for peace rapidly evaporated and the violence continued on both sides.

The U.S. Call for New Palestinian Leadership

Israel's intensified crackdown on Palestinians gained U.S. support after September 11, 2001, when the U.S.-led war on terrorism began. Thereafter, Israel equated its attacks on Palestinian militant groups with the U.S. drive to find and destroy terrorists around the world. Israel also claimed Arafat was unwilling to stop Palestinian terror, and in December 2001 Israel called him "irrelevant" to any peace process.

Arafat's image was further tarnished in January 2002, just a few months after the September 11 attacks, when Israel dis-

President George Bush explains his vision for Middle East peace in June 2002. This vision included both an independent Palestinian state and new Palestinian leadership.

covered Arafat's involvement in an illegal PLO arms shipment containing fifty tons of Iranian weapons, including rockets, antitank missiles, land mines, sniper rifles, mortar shells, and explosives. The discovery revealed that Arafat, despite his renunciation of terrorism, still pursued armed conflict with Israel. The incident irrevocably damaged Arafat's relationship with the United States, which took actions to further isolate him.

On June 24, 2002, citing Arafat's ineffectiveness, Bush announced that U.S. support for eventual Palestinian independence required new Palestinian leadership. Urging all parties in the Middle East to "break with the past and set out on a new path," Bush stated: "Peace requires a new and different Palestinian leadership, so that a Palestinian state can be born. I call on the Palestinian people to elect new leaders, leaders not compromised by terror. I call upon them to build a practicing democracy, based on tolerance and liberty."[34]

Bush also laid out his vision for Middle East peace based on two states living side by side in peace and security and promised, "When the Palestinian people have new leaders, new institutions and new security arrangements with their neighbors, the United States of America will support the creation of a Palestinian state." At the same time, Bush called on Israel to withdraw its forces from Palestinian areas it occupied following the start of the second Palestinian intifada on September 28, 2000, and declared that "Israeli settlement activity in the occupied territories must stop."[35]

The United States began working with the European Union, Russia, and the United Nations (what became known as the "Quartet") to develop a detailed "road map" to guide Israel and the Palestinians toward peace. In addition, in July 2002 an international Task Force on Palestinian Reform was established to monitor and support Palestinian reforms. Thereafter, America's push for war on Iraq diverted U.S. attention for several months. In February 2003, however, President Bush said progress was being made on the road map. Once again, he emphasized that "[a] Palestinian state must be a reformed and peaceful state that abandons forever the use of terror" and that "Israel . . . will be expected to support the creation of a viable Palestinian state and to work as quickly as possible toward a final status agreement."[36]

Palestinian Reforms

Palestinian leaders appeared to heed Bush's calls for reform, partly because Palestinians themselves had become disillusioned with Arafat's leadership and wanted reform. As a result of both external and internal pressures, therefore, the Palestinian Authority (PA) began drafting a constitution that would embody the democratic principles, such as separation of powers, outlined by the United States. Also, at the urging of the United States and Israel, the Palestinian Authority elected a new, more independent cabinet and created a new post of prime minister to dilute Arafat's power.

Although Arafat initially opposed him, a moderate Palestinian, Mahmoud Abbas, was appointed as prime minister in April 2003. Abbas was opposed to the

The Palestinian Economic Crisis

The second intifada, in which Palestinians violently protested Israeli occupation of Palestinian territories, has led to Israeli military and security responses that destroy Palestinian lives and properties. A March 2003 report by the World Bank, for example, concluded that the intifada has caused a dramatic decline in all economic indicators. The report said that physical damage from the conflict, as of the end of August 2002, was as much as $728 million. Unemployment in 2003 was estimated at 53 percent of the Palestinian population. Business activity, meanwhile, has plummeted; Palestinian exports since the start of the intifada have declined 45 percent and imports have been reduced by one-third.

The main cause of the Palestinian economic crisis, the report said, was the Israeli government's restriction of goods and services across borders and within the occupied territories. These restrictions include curfews that restrict Palestinian activities within the territories and border closures, which prevent Palestinian workers from entering Israel. The impact of the crisis on ordinary Palestinians, the report said, was serious. To survive, families have had to sell their assets, borrow from others, and rely on food aid. Millions live in poverty and there is an increase in health problems, malnutrition, violent behavior in schools, and hopelessness.

Palestinian children wait in line for food. The second intifada and Israel's response to the attacks has led to an economic crisis in the occupied territories.

intifada and other means of Palestinian violence as a means of achieving peace, and in favor of a land-for-peace deal. However, Abbas may have had more support in the United States and Israel than among Palestinians, who believed he was too accommodating to Israel. Also, Abbas's clout over Palestinian militia groups such as Hamas was weak, and so he could not do much to rein in violence.

In addition to changes in leadership, the PA made other significant reforms. Indeed, the Task Force on Palestinian Reform, composed of representatives of the Quartet, Norway, Japan, Canada, the World Bank, and the International Monetary Fund, met in London in February 2003 and concluded that the Palestinians had made "clear and considerable progress"[37] in several areas. For example, the Task Force praised the PA's implementation of economic and financial reforms and in particular noted the Palestinian Legislative Council's approval of a fully funded 2003 Palestinian budget, which provided necessary social and emergency services, financial support for Palestinian municipalities, and payments on PA debts.

Abbas's election and the other reforms put in place by the PA renewed hopes in America and Israel that it might be possible to negotiate with the Palestinians, setting the stage for another round of peace talks.

CHAPTER 6

Possibilities for Peace

Buoyed by the changes in the Palestinian leadership and America's victory in the war against Iraq, President Bush in April 2003 released a new Middle East peace plan, called the Road Map. As a result of Bush's initiative, a temporary cease-fire was implemented by Palestinians and talks began between the two sides. It was a good beginning, but talks soon were disrupted by renewed violence. It remains to be seen whether a permanent peace between Israelis and Palestinians will be achievable given the astounding violence and pain both sides have endured.

The Road Map
The Road Map is a performance-based, goal-oriented plan with a clear timeline and benchmarks. It proposes a three-phase process to be completed by 2005.

Phase one seeks to reestablish security in the occupied areas. It also requires mutual statements from Palestinian and Israel leadership calling for an end to violence, recognizing Israel's right to exist, and reiterating Israel's commitment to an independent Palestinian state. In addition, during phase one, Palestinians are required to draft a constitution for Palestinian statehood and conduct free elections. Israel is required to withdraw from Palestinian areas it occupied during the al-Aqsa intifada, freeze settlements, dismantle new settlement outposts, and improve the Palestinian humanitarian situation.

The goal of phase two is to establish a Palestinian state with provisional borders. This state is to be independent, antiterror, and democratic. In addition, an international conference is to be held to aid Palestinian economic recovery and discuss multilateral Middle East issues, such as water, environment, economic development, refugees, and arms control issues. Phase three involves negotiating a final peace settlement and permanent borders for the new Palestinian nation; these negotiations are to begin by 2005. Thereafter, a second international conference is to be held to approve the final peace agreement and encourage peace treaties between Israel and the two remaining hostile Arab states—Syria and Lebanon.

The Palestinians accepted the Road Map soon after it was announced. Although the Israeli government raised fourteen objections to the plan, Israel's cabinet voted to accept it on May 25, 2003, marking the first time in history that the Israeli government formally accepted the idea of a Palestinian state.

The Road Map Crashes

Following their acceptance of the Road Map, both sides made hopeful statements and took symbolic actions to move the peace process forward. For example, in a May meeting of the Likud Party's parliamentary members, Sharon shocked many in Israel by describing the Israeli action in Palestinian areas for the first time as an "occupation" of the West Bank and Gaza Strip. (Many Israelis see Israel's presence in the territories as a legitimate claim to Jewish land, and not as an occupation of Arab land.) He said, "You cannot like the word, but what is happening is an occupation—to hold 3.5

Release of Palestinian Prisoners

One of the demands from Palestinians during the early stages of the 2003 Road Map was for Israel to release the thousands of Palestinians held in Israeli jails. The Palestinians object to Israel's practice of arresting so many Palestinians, many of whom get rounded up by Israel simply because they protest Israel's occupation and oppression policies. Israel, however, is usually reluctant to release prisoners, because many are considered to be active terrorists or sympathetic to Palestinian terrorism.

In July 2003, however, Sharon announced that Israel would release a total of 540 Palestinian prisoners, including 210 prisoners from Hamas and Islamic Jihad, 210 linked to al-Fatah and the PLO, and 120 common criminals. Israel agreed to release these prisoners because all of them had been convicted of relatively minor crimes or were being held by Israel without being charged. A short time later, however, Israel released only about 350 prisoners. Palestinians, who wanted a release of all 6,000 Palestinians held in Israeli jails, considered the release totally inadequate. Palestinians also pointed out that 31 of the released prisoners were about to complete their sentences, which means they would have been released soon anyway. The prisoner release issue stalled completely following the renewed violence that culminated in the end of the cease-fire and cessation of peace negotiations.

million Palestinians under occupation. I believe that is a terrible thing for Israel and for the Palestinians."[38]

For his part, Abbas was successful in getting Palestinian militia groups like Hamas and Islamic Jihad to declare a temporary, ninety-day truce to the intifada, sharply decreasing the violence in the occupied territories. Sharon, in turn, responded by withdrawing troops from northern Gaza and Bethlehem. He also announced that Israel would take down a limited number of Jewish settlements that had been established without government authorization. As of July 2003 about a dozen such unauthorized settlements had been removed, with another fifty to go. The nearly 150 government-

Palestinians surround the site where Hamas leader Ismail Abu Shanab was killed by Israeli forces in August 2003.

approved settlements, Sharon said, would stay until the final stages of peace talks.

However, the cease-fire quickly collapsed amid a renewed spiral of violence from both sides. The most serious setback for the cease-fire occurred on August 19, 2003, when a suicide bomber blew up a bus in Jerusalem full of families, killing twenty and wounding over one hundred, many of them children. Hamas claimed responsibility for the bombing, saying it was in revenge for Israel's earlier killing of Hamas members.

In response to the bombing, Israel immediately suspended talks with the Palestinians and arrested seventeen suspects in a raid into Hebron, the bomber's hometown. Abbas, meanwhile, ordered Palestinian security services to arrest the militants behind the bombing. However, before the Palestinians took action, Israel on August 21 sent helicopter gunships to kill Hamas leader Ismail Abu Shanab as he drove through Gaza City.

Fed up with suicide attacks, Israel continued to assassinate Hamas leaders in 2004. On March 22, 2004, IDF forces assassinated Hamas's spiritual leader, Sheikh Ahmed Yassin for continuing to inspire suicide bombers. Missiles fired from an Israeli helicopter killed Yassin, along with seven other Palestinians. Less than a month later, Israel assassinated his replacement, Abdel Aziz Rantissi. Rantissi had cofounded Hamas and was an outspoken opponent of the state of Israel. On April 17, 2004, Israeli helicopters fired two missiles into a white sedan that was carrying the new Hamas leader through the Gaza Strip, killing him and two others, including his son. As news of Rantissi's death spread, tens of thousands of furious Palestinians swarmed to the streets, vowing revenge for both of the assassinations.

Hamas also promised to avenge the deaths, and both Hamas and Islamic Jihad declared the cease-fire over. Ismail al-Haniyah, a Hamas spokesman, said, "The Zionist enemy has assassinated the truce and the Hamas movement holds the Zionist enemy fully responsible for the consequences of its crime."[39] As of summer 2004 the cease-fire, and possibly the Road Map peace process itself, appeared to be dead.

Prospects for the Road Map became even worse when Abbas submitted his resignation as Palestinian prime minister. Abbas's action left the Palestinian Authority once again under the full control of Yasir Arafat, a leader whom neither Israel nor the United States is willing to accept. Arafat named a new prime minister, Ahmed Qurei, to replace Abbas, but how long Qurei would keep the position seemed unclear by spring of 2004.

Security for Israel

Even if Israel and the Palestinians are able to revive the cease-fire and resume peace talks under the Road Map, they face a host of difficult issues before the two sides can succeed in negotiating a permanent peace treaty. One of the most important initial issues, for Israel, is security. In one of its objections to the Road Map, Israel demanded that the Palestinians, as part of phase one, combat terror by completely dismantling Palestinian terrorist organizations such as Hamas, Islamic Jihad, the Democratic Front, and the Al-Aqsa Brigades. Israel believes that peace talks cannot be held amid continuing suicide bombings, and it is unwilling to go forward in negotiations until its citizens are protected from this threat.

Many Palestinians, however, view Hamas and similar groups as freedom fighters for the Palestinian cause and suicide bombings their only effective way of striking back at Israel for its occupation of Palestinian lands. Giving up this weapon before Israel makes any real concessions in the peace process has been unacceptable to the Palestinian side. In addition, only Arafat seems to have enough power to control these groups, but he has either been unable or unwilling to do so. Hamas and Islamic Jihad typically reject making any peace with Israel, as they do not believe it has the right to exist. Thus, when Arafat begins to make peace concessions, the extremist groups will conduct terrorist acts to sabotage the entire process. An effective way to halt the operations of Hamas and other extremist groups has not yet been found.

Another action Israel began taking to increase its security after the wave of Palestinian suicide bombings was the building of a security barrier in the West Bank. This barrier, called a fence by Israel and a wall by Palestinians, is made of concrete, razor wire, trenches, sensors, and cameras, and is hundreds of feet high. It is designed to prevent Palestinians from crossing into Israeli settlements and across Israel's borders, and most Israelis support it as the only way to stop terrorist attacks. As writer Ari Shavit describes, "It is a tragic project.

. . . It looks like the Berlin Wall. . . . But there is a lot to be said in defense of the wall. . . . This is the Israeli people's reaction to the intifada and the suicide bombing. What the wall says is that we want to have our coastline democracy—a small, sane, quiet country of our own, keeping both the Palestinians and the settlers out."[40]

The wall/fence was not addressed specifically by the Road Map but is considered a major obstacle to peace by Palestinians. The Palestinians object to it because the wall is not being built on the 1967 border between Israel and the Palestinian territories. Instead, it will stretch 225 miles within the West Bank, absorbing more Palestinian land into Israel. Also, it separates many Palestinian farmers from their fields and meanders in a way that suppresses travel and commerce. It also almost completely surrounds many Palestinian villages, creating what appear to be Palestinian cages and oppressing ordinary Palestinians more than ever before. Perhaps most importantly, Palestinians fear that Israel intends for the barrier to become the permanent border between Israel and Palestine.

As of fall 2003 only about one-fifth of the barrier had been completed, mainly along the northern and western borders between the West Bank and Israel. If Israel continues building the wall, it will intrude deep into the West Bank to protect Jewish settlements, and will virtually imprison many Palestinians. The United States, Israeli peace proponents, and Palestinians have urged Sharon to halt construction of the barrier, and the United States threatened to make deductions from a $9 billion package of

Palestinians object to the building of this security barrier between Israel and the West Bank. Israelis believe it is the only way to ensure their safety from suicide attacks.

loans if Israel pursued the wall strategy. In September 2003, however, the Israeli cabinet made its choice: It approved extending the wall into the West Bank.

Improved Living Conditions for Palestinians

Also essential to peace is the reconstruction of many Palestinian areas destroyed or damaged by Israeli raids during the intifada. Many say that if Israel helps with aid and reconstruction efforts, it will be proof of its goodwill and give Palestinians hope and faith in the peace process.

In July 2003 Bush announced that the United States would provide $20 million in direct financial assistance to the Palestinian Authority to help relieve Palestinian poverty. He indicated the United States was prepared to provide up to $300 million in aid to Palestine to repair the damage done by Israeli armed forces. Bush also urged Israel "to take further steps to improve the daily conditions faced by Palestinians," explaining, "Israelis and Palestinians deserve the same chance to live normal lives free from fear, free from hatred and violence and free from harassment."[41]

Specifically, the United States asked Israel to take actions such as relaxing border closures and checkpoints, releasing more prisoners, and dismantling approximately one hundred settlements built in recent years.

Israel, however, continued to maintain that it could not take these steps until the Palestinian Authority took concrete actions to improve Israel's security—like making arrests and seizing arms from militants. Palestinians also continued their complaints that the United States helped the two sides disproportionately, favoring Israel in negotiations, aid packages, and weapons sales.

Removal of Israeli Settlements

Still another issue that lies at the heart of future peace negotiations is whether Israel will agree to remove Israeli settlements from the occupied territories of

The Right of Return

Another issue important to Palestinians is how to deal with hundreds of thousands of Palestinian refugees created as a result of the 1948 war and thereafter. Today, about 2.5 million refugees live in refugee camps in Jordan, Syria, and Lebanon. The Palestinians insist on a "right of return" for all these refugees. They argue that this right is protected by international law and is supported by UN Resolution 194, which calls for displaced refugees to be allowed to return to their homes under certain circumstances. The Palestinians assert that any peace deal with Israel must include not only the right of every refugee to return to his or her home in Israel, but also compensation from Israel to the refugees for loss or damage to property, personal injury, and mental pain and anguish.

Israel flatly refuses any such idea of refugee return, claiming that a large number of returnees would swamp Israel, perhaps even establish an Arab majority in Israel—a possibility that would create intense political problems. Israel was founded as a Jewish state to provide refuge to Jewish people, and Israelis fear that allowing all Palestinian refugees and their descendants, many of whom would have anti-Jewish political views, to return home, would mean that Israel would cease to exist as a Jewish state.

Most Israelis believe that because the Arab countries declared war on Israel after it announced its independence, it is the Arab countries who are responsible for the fact that there were refugees at all and who therefore should have absorbed them. At Taba, Israel informally floated the idea of allowing a small number of refugees, perhaps twenty-five thousand, into Israel as part of a family reunion program. Other ideas include the payment of compensation to refugees in lieu of allowing them to return. However, many observers see the Palestinian insistence on refugee return as an unrealistic demand, given today's facts and political climate.

Israeli soldiers and Jewish settlers clash as Israel prepares to dismantle a West Bank settlement in March 2004.

the West Bank and Gaza. As of February 2002 there were a total of about four hundred thousand Israelis living in the occupied territories. Some settlements are quite small, with only a few hundred inhabitants and surrounded by empty space. Others, however, are the size of large towns or small cities; Ma'aleh Ad-

umim, a settlement east of Jerusalem, for example, has a population of twenty-eight thousand.

Palestinians view the settlements as an illegal landgrab by the Israelis. To build the settlements, Israel confiscated some of the best agricultural land available to Palestinians while exhausting Palestinian water sources. Also, the settlements are scattered throughout the occupied territories; they are connected by Israeli roads and checkpoints and are protected by the Israeli military. Thus the settlements divide Palestinian areas and hinder transportation, commerce, and freedom of movement for Palestinians. Palestinians want all settlements removed, so that land in the occupied territories can be absorbed into an independent Palestinian state.

Israel, however, maintains that it has a right to establish settlements in the territories because it won them in the 1967 Six-Day War. Also, some Israelis believe Jews have a religious right to settle in the West Bank, called Judea and Samaria in the Bible, because much of ancient Jewish history took place there. These Israelis have used Jewish settlements as a way to establish and maintain Israeli control over the occupied territories. Israelis, however, are divided on the issue. Some openly promote the settlements as part of a strategy to ensure that the territories seized in 1967 are never given back to the Palestinians. Others, however, disapprove of the settlement policy and see the necessity of trading land (and settlements) for peace with the Palestinians.

The Road Map requires Israel in phase one to dismantle settlement outposts established during the intifada and freeze new settlements. Prime Minister Sharon, however, who has been a strong proponent of expanding settlements throughout his career, resisted U.S. pressures to stop or reverse settlement activity. In an approach that ran contrary to the terms of the Road Map, Sharon agreed in phase one only to dismantle a small number of what he called "unauthorized" settlements, leaving many settlement outposts established by Israel during the intifada. He also refused to halt new settlements, instead allowing the Jewish settler population to grow by more than five thousand in the first half of 2003. In addition, Israel announced plans to build more than six hundred new homes in existing Jewish settlements.

For a final peace, however, the Road Map calls for Israel to remove settlements from the occupied territories in exchange for Arab recognition of the right of Israel to live in peace. Accordingly, peace proposals over the years have suggested Israel withdraw from most settlements and the Palestinians from any settlement areas that Israel does not leave. At the Taba peace talks in 2001, for example, Israel proposed that 6 percent of the occupied territories become part of Israel, with an exchange of other Israeli lands. Palestinians countered with an offer of 3 percent. If the parties had been able to agree at Taba, the deal could have given the Palestinians as much as 97 percent of the land in the West Bank for their independent state. The Taba talks, therefore, may provide a moderate starting point for future negotiations on territory.

The land-for-peace compromise, although supported by many Israelis and Palestinians, is a highly controversial issue and leaders on both sides face extremists who are opposed to moderate solutions. Coming to a satisfactory agreement on this issue will be one of the most difficult negotiations facing the two sides.

Sharing the City of Jerusalem

Of all the areas in the occupied territories, the most important to both Israelis and Palestinians is the city of Jerusalem—this city that has deep religious significance to Jews, Christians, and Muslims. Jerusalem lies on the border between Israel and the West Bank; indeed, it is divided between West Jerusalem, which lies squarely in Israel, and East Jerusalem, which falls in the West Bank region. In particular, an area of the city known as the Old City is important because it contains most of the sites viewed as holy by both religions. For Jews, it is the site of the Jewish temple, called the Temple Mount, including the western wall of the temple, called the Wailing Wall. For Muslims, Jerusalem is the third most important holy place in Islam and the site of the Dome of the Rock, which is the location of the mosque of al-Aqsa, an important Muslim mosque.

The city of Jerusalem and its holy sites, such as the Wailing Wall and the Dome of the Rock (pictured), hold great religious significance for both Israelis and Palestinians.

Jerusalem is claimed by both Israel and the Palestinians as their capital. Early in Israel's modern history, Jerusalem was divided, its western half coming under Israeli control and its eastern side under Jordanian control. In the 1967 war, Israel captured East Jerusalem, gaining control over all of the city. Afterward, Israel expanded Jerusalem's boundaries and built numerous Israeli settlements around the city. Since 1993 Israel has closed Jerusalem, restricting access to Palestinians. Palestinians claim this closure policy has kept them from visiting their holy sites in Jerusalem, even during religious holidays, and also has isolated an important economic and cultural center from the rest of the West Bank.

The Palestinians insist that East Jerusalem be returned to them and that Jerusalem become the capital of an independent Palestinian state. Israelis are reluctant to give up control over sacred

Arab Support for Palestinian Terrorism

Arab nations have historically voiced support for the Palestinian cause, but they do not speak with a united voice. Some Arab nations, for example, agreed to support the Road Map plan for peace by cutting off funding to Palestinian terrorist groups. For example, as quoted by CNN at a June 2003 meeting attended by U.S. president Bush and leaders from Saudi Arabia, Jordan, and Bahrain, Egyptian president Hosni Mubarak promised, "We will use the full force of the law to stop funds getting to illegal organizations including terrorist groups."

Mubarak, however, was speaking only for those four Arab nations at the June meeting, not for the eighteen other Arab nations. Some of the less moderate Arab states never gave their support to the Bush peace initiative, have not made peace with Israel, and are suspected of continuing their funding of Palestinian terrorist groups. Syria, for example, has been a key supporter of pro-Palestinian terrorists. Syria has said it will not make peace with Israel until Israel pulls out of the Golan Heights, an area in southern Syria that was occupied by Israel in the 1967 war and later annexed, or formally made part of, Israel.

In 2003, however, following the U.S.-Iraq war, Syria signaled a change in its policies. It sought to renew peace negotiations with Israel, agreed not to interfere in the Road Map negotiations process for a Palestinian solution, and pledged it will no longer provide arms to Hizballah, one of the pro-Palestinian militia groups based in Lebanon. It is unclear, however, whether Syria has fulfilled these promises. Indeed, in October 2003 Israel bombed a target inside Syria that it claimed was an Islamic Jihad training base, accusing Syria of continuing its support for terrorist organizations. Also, Lebanon, another Arab state that shares borders with Israel, has yet to show a willingness to support the Road Map or make peace with Israel. Instead, Lebanon still supports the Palestinian intifada, and Hizballah militants based in Lebanon continue to attack Israel.

Jewish areas such as the Temple Mount and assert they must retain control of all of Jerusalem, undivided. At Taba, Israel proposed the creation of a special international zone for older parts of the city containing religious sites, but Palestinians insisted on Palestinian sovereignty instead. Because of the emotion attached to this issue on both sides, the sharing of Jerusalem will be one of the most contentious issues facing Israel and the Palestinians in any future peace negotiations.

The Future for Peace

The future for Middle East peace, as of summer 2004, appeared uncertain. The collapse of the Road Map peace initiative, the continuation of the intifada, and the long history of failed attempts to move toward a permanent peace treaty between Israel and the Palestinians certainly does not bode well for success. The absence of effective, moderate leadership on the Palestinian side, combined with the hard-line use of force by leaders on the Israeli side, has produced a stalemate that points only to more violence and to greater suffering for both Israelis and Palestinians.

Despite the setbacks, however, a number of factors suggest that peace may eventually be achieved. First, the broad outlines of a two-state solution, in which Israel pulls out of the West Bank and Gaza and the Palestinians establish an independent state in those areas, have been discussed for many years. This plan has support from most of the international community. Second, although marked by many failures and unimaginable suffering, the peace process has moved forward in recent decades, inching closer and closer to a final settlement. The next time the two sides are able to formally negotiate, the agenda will be permanent peace issues. Third, Israel has been able to maintain a lasting peace with several Arab nations; it is hoped that a permanent peace with all Arab states can eventually be achieved, thus concluding the Arab-Israeli conflict.

Also, in one sense, time may be running out for an Israeli-Palestinian peace agreement, because some have suggested that the Palestinians may soon simply give up seeking a Palestinian state and demand Israeli citizenship and voting rights. Such a development would be disasterous for Israel because the high birth rate of Palestinians by 2020 may cause Palestinians to outnumber Jews in Israeli-controlled areas. If this happens, there would be more Palestinians than Israelis in Israel. Israel will then be hard-pressed to allow its Jewish minority to rule an Arab majority. As a *New York Times* editorial stated, "The conclusion is clear. Israel must begin to plan its exit from the West Bank and Gaza not only to permit the creation of a viable, contiguous Palestinian state but to preserve its own future."[42]

With so many controversial and emotionally charged issues, the road ahead for Israel and the Arabs of the region remains indeed perilous. As their history has so often proven, peace negotiations all too easily become the victim of extremist violence. Whether visionary leadership will emerge to restart the peace process, or whether it will unravel into another cycle of tit-for-tat violence, no one knows.

NOTES

Chapter 1: Roots of the Conflict

1. Quoted in Ian J. Bickerton and Carla L. Klausner, *A Concise History of the Arab-Israeli Conflict*. Upper Saddle River, NJ: Prentice-Hall, 2002, p. 35.
2. Quoted in Samih K. Farsoun and Christina E. Zacharia, *Palestine and the Palestinians*. Boulder, CO: Westview, 1997, p. 72.
3. Quoted in Bickerton and Klausner, *A Concise History of the Arab-Israeli Conflict*, p. 44.
4. Quoted in Farsoun and Zacharia, *Palestine and the Palestinians*, p. 74.
5. Quoted in Farsoun and Zacharia, *Palestine and the Palestinians*, p. 71.
6. Farsoun and Zacharia, *Palestine and the Palestinians*, pp. 74–75.
7. Ahron Bregman, *Israel's Wars: A History Since 1947*. New York: Routledge, 2002, p. 9.
8. Quoted in Bickerton and Klausner, *A Concise History of the Arab-Israeli Conflict*, p. 56.
9. Bickerton and Klausner, *A Concise History of the Arab-Israeli Conflict*, p. 70.

Chapter 2: The Arab-Israeli Wars

10. Mark Tessler, *A History of the Israeli-Palestinian Conflict*. Bloomington: Indiana University Press, 1994, p. 273.
11. Rashid Khalidi, "The Palestinians and 1948: The Underlying Causes of Failure," in *The War for Palestine*, Eugene L. Rogan and Avi Shlaim, eds., New York: Cambridge University Press, 2001, p. 12.
12. Bickerton and Klausner, *A Concise History of the Arab-Israeli Conflict*, p. 151.
13. Farsoun and Zacharia, *Palestine and the Palestinians*, p. 183.
14. Farsoun and Zacharia, *Palestine and the Palestinians*, p. 189.

Chapter 3: The Palestinians Rise Up

15. Quoted in Tessler, *A History of the Israeli-Palestinian Conflict*, p. 506.
16. Tessler, *A History of the Israeli-Palestinian Conflict*, p. 564.
17. Quoted in Tessler, *A History of the Israeli-Palestinian Conflict*, p. 638.
18. Farsoun and Zacharia, *Palestine and the Palestinians*, p. 214.

19. Farsoun and Zacharia, *Palestine and the Palestinians*, p. 245.

Chapter 4: Turning Toward Peace

20. Quoted in Farsoun and Zacharia, *Palestine and the Palestinians*, p. 244.
21. Ahron Bregman and Jihan el-Tahri, *The Fifty Years' War: Israel and the Arabs*. New York: TV Books, 1999, p. 273.
22. Martin Gilbert, *Israel: A History*. New York: William Morrow, 1998, p. 565.
23. Quoted in Farsoun and Zacharia, *Palestine and the Palestinians*, p. 257.
24. Farsoun and Zacharia, *Palestine and the Palestinians*, p. 267.
25. Quoted in Farsoun and Zacharia, *Palestine and the Palestinians*, p. 291.
26. Baruch Kimmerling, *Politicide: Ariel Sharon's War Against the Palestinians*. New York: Verso, 2003, p. 136.
27. Quoted in Gilbert, *Israel*, p. 587.
28. Quoted in Bregman and el-Tahri, *The Fifty Years' War*, p. 339.
29. Quoted in Palestine Facts, "What Took Place at Camp David in 2000?" www.palestinefacts.org.

Chapter 5: The Conflict Continues

30. Haim Gordon, Rivca Gordon, and Taher Shriteh, *Beyond Intifada: Narratives of Freedom Fighters in the Gaza Strip*. Westport, CT: Praeger, 2003, p. 130.
31. Quoted in Gordon, Gordon, and Shriteh, *Beyond Intifada*, p. 131.
32. Quoted in Kimmerling, *Politicide*, p. 166.
33. Efraim Karsh, "What Occupation?" *Commentary*, July–August 2002.
34. George W. Bush, remarks by the president on the Middle East, the White House, Washington, D.C., July 24, 2002. http://usinfo.state.gov.
35. Bush, remarks on the Middle East.
36. George W. Bush, speech at the American Enterprise Institute in Washington, D.C., February 26, 2003. http://usinfo.state.gov.
37. U.S. News Service, "Statement of the Task Force on Palestinian Reform," February 20, 2003. www.reliefweb.int/w/rwb.nsf.

Chapter 6: Possibilities for Peace

38. Quoted in Kelly Wallace, "Sharon: 'Occupation' Terrible for Israel, Palestinians," CNN, May 27, 2003. www.cnn.com.
39. Quoted in Reuters, "Islamic Militant Groups Say Truce Dead After Israeli Strike," *New York Times*, August 21, 2003.
40. Quoted in Thomas L. Friedman, "One Wall, One Man, One Vote," *New York Times*, September 15, 2003.
41. Quoted in Associated Press, "Sharon Defends Security Fence That Bush Has Criticized," *New York Times*, July 29, 2003.
42. *New York Times*, "Middle East Math," September 12, 2003.

CHRONOLOGY

A.D. 70
The Romans capture Jerusalem, exile most Jewish inhabitants.

644
Palestine becomes an Islamic/Arab state.

1517
The Ottoman Empire conquers Palestine.

1897
Theodor Herzl founds the World Zionist Movement.

1917
Britain issues the Balfour Declaration. At the end of World War I, Britain invades Palestine and establishes a military occupation.

1928
Between 1914 and 1928, over one hundred thousand Jews immigrate to Palestine.

1930
Britain issues the Passfield White Paper, halting Jewish immigration, but this policy is reversed a year later by British prime minister MacDonald.

1935–36
Arabs revolt against Britain and its Zionist policies.

1937
The Peel Commission recommends that Palestine be divided into separate Jewish and Arab states.

1939
World War II begins. Britain issues the White Paper, which restricts Jewish immigration and proposes that Palestine become an independent state within ten years.

1941–45
The German Nazis conduct the Holocaust, seeking to destroy all Jews in Europe.

1945
World War II ends. Jewish militant groups revolt against the British in Palestine.

1946
Anglo-American Committee of Inquiry recommends that one hundred thousand Jews be admitted into Palestine and that the area become a binational state for both Jews and Arabs.

1947
The United Nations votes to partition Palestine into two states, one Jewish and one Arab.

1948

May 14: Britain officially terminates its mandate in Palestine and leaves the area. That same day, Israel declares its independence, and the War of Independence begins when five Arab states—Egypt, Jordan, Syria, Lebanon, and Iraq—invade Palestine.

1949

Israel and the Arab states sign an armistice ending the War of Independence.

1955

After an Israeli attack on an Egyptian military post in Gaza, Egyptian president Nasser sets up commando training camps to train Palestinian fedayeen fighters.

1956

October 29: Israel, France, and Britain attack Egypt, starting the Suez/Sinai War.

1964

The Palestine Liberation Organization (PLO) is formed.

1967

June 5: Israel attacks Egypt, beginning the Six Day War. Israel captures Arab territories in Gaza, the Sinai Peninsula, Jerusalem, the West Bank, and the Golan Heights.

1968

Yasir Arafat becomes leader of the PLO, which then becomes the representative for most of the various Palestinian guerrilla groups.

1973

October 6: Egyptian and Syrian forces attack Israel, starting the Yom Kippur War.

1974

The United Nations recognizes the PLO as the Palestinian representative and invites Yasir Arafat to speak.

1975

U.S. secretary of state Henry Kissinger negotiates an end to the Yom Kippur War and return of Egyptian and Syrian land seized during the war by Israel.

1978

Following negotiations, Israel and Egypt sign peace agreements called the Camp David Accords, which provide for a self-governing elected Arab authority in the West Bank and Gaza and the return of Sinai to Egypt.

1979

Israel and Egypt sign a formal peace treaty.

1982

June 6: Israel invades Lebanon seeking to destroy the PLO headquarters there.

1987

December 8: An Israeli military vehicle strikes cars at a military checkpoint in Gaza, killing Palestinians and starting a mass Palestinian uprising called the intifada.

1988

King Hussein of Jordan announces Jordan will no longer administer the West

Bank. Arafat renounces terrorism and recognizes Israel's right to exist.

1990
Iraq invades Kuwait, leading to the Persian Gulf War.

1991
October 20: U.S. president George Herbert Walker Bush opens a peace conference in Madrid, Spain, which is attended by Israel and the Arab states.

1992
Yitzhak Rabin is elected as Israeli prime minister.

1993
Arafat and Rabin resume formal peace talks, and secret peace talks begin in Oslo, Norway. The secret talks result in the signing on September 13 of the Oslo Agreement, giving Palestinians self-rule.

1994
October 26: Jordan and Israel sign a formal peace treaty.

1995
September 28: A second peace agreement, the Oslo II Agreement, is signed, creating the Palestinian Authority and giving it full control over Palestinians.

November 4: A Jewish religious zealot assassinates Israeli prime minister Yitzhak Rabin, and Benjamin Netanyahu is elected prime minister.

1996
Arafat is elected as president of the Palestinian Authority.

1997
Netanyahu and Arafat continue the Oslo peace process, and Netanyahu loses support in Israel.

1999
Ehud Barak is elected Israeli prime minister by promising to revive peace talks.

2000
July: Peace talks are held at Camp David, Maryland; a summit meeting between President Clinton, Arafat, and Barak, but talks collapse after Arafat rejects proposal by Israel without offering a counterproposal.

September 28: Ariel Sharon visits the Temple Mount, sparking the second intifada.

2001
Sharon elected prime minister in a landslide.

2002
March 28: A suicide bomber blows himself up at a hotel during the Jewish holiday of Passover, killing twenty-eight.

March 29: Israel begins Operation Defensive Shield, reoccupying Palestinian towns in the West Bank.

June 24: President George W. Bush calls on Palestinians to replace Arafat as the Palestinian leader.

January 28: Sharon is reelected prime minister of Israel.

2003
April 30: Mahmoud Abbas takes office as the Palestinian prime minister.

May 1: The Road Map peace plan is presented.

June 29: Palestinian groups (Fatah, Hamas, and Islamic Jihad) announce a three-month cease-fire and vow to stop attacks against Israelis. Israel pulls troops back from the northern Gaza Strip and the two sides begin to implement the Road Map, with U.S. president George W. Bush acting as mediator.

August 21: The cease-fire ends following a Hamas suicide bomber attack on a bus in Jerusalem that kills twenty and Israel's retaliatory killing of a Hamas leader.

September 6: Abbas submits his resignation as Palestinian prime minister. Arafat names a new prime minister, Ahmed Qurei, to replace Abbas.

October 5: Israel bombs a target inside Syria, claiming it was an Islamic Jihad training base.

FOR FURTHER READING

Books

David J. Abodaher, *Youth in the Middle East: Voices of Despair*. New York: Franklin Watts, 1990. Conversations with young people in the Middle East. They describe the political situation there and how it has affected them.

Elizabeth Ferber, *Yasir Arafat: A Life of War and Peace*. Brookfield, CT: Millbrook, 1995. A biography of Yasir Arafat.

Laurel Holliday, *Why Do They Hate Me? Young Lives Caught in War and Conflict*. New York: Pocket Books, 1999. A collection of nonfiction essays about children in violent conflicts such as the Holocaust and the Israeli-Palestinian war.

Gloria D. Miklowitz, *The Enemy Has a Face*. Grand Rapids, MI: Eerdmans, 2003. A fictional tale about a girl from Israel who believes her brother has been kidnapped by Palestinian terrorists.

Ann Morris, *When Will the Fighting Stop? A Child's View of Jerusalem*. New York: Atheneum, 1990. A story about a Jewish boy living in Jerusalem who wonders why all the people living in the city cannot be friends.

Internet Sources

International Information Programs, U.S. Department of State, "The Middle East: A Vision for the Future." http://usinfo.state.gov.

Israel Ministry of Foreign Affairs, "The Peace Process." www.mfa.gov.il.

Mideast Web, "Middle East History and Resources." www.mideastweb.org.

Web Sites

Foundation for Middle East Peace (www.fmep.org). A site run by a nonprofit organization dedicated to informing Americans about the Israeli-Palestinian conflict and assisting in a peaceful solution that brings security for both sides.

Israel/Palestine Center for Research and Information (www.ipcri.org). This is a joint Palestinian-Israeli public policy think tank that seeks to develop practical solutions for the Israeli-Palestinian conflict.

WORKS CONSULTED

Books

Ian J. Bickerton and Carla L. Klausner, *A Concise History of the Arab-Israeli Conflict*. Upper Saddle River, NJ: Prentice-Hall, 2002. A short but substantive history of the Arab-Israeli conflict from the time of Ottoman rule to the election of Ariel Sharon as prime minister of Israel.

Ahron Bregman, *Israel's Wars: A History Since 1947*. New York: Routledge, 2002. An account of Israel's wars with the Palestinians and the Arabs.

Ahron Bregman and Jihan el-Tahri, *The Fifty Years' War: Israel and the Arabs*. New York: TV Books, 1999. An entertaining account of the conflict between Jews and Arabs through the 1987 intifada, with revealing behind-the-scenes eyewitness insights.

Samih K. Farsoun and Christina E. Zacharia, *Palestine and the Palestinians*. Boulder, CO: Westview, 1997. This book provides an analysis of the political development of the Palestine people from early times to their modern demands for statehood.

Martin Gilbert, *Israel: A History*. New York: William Morrow, 1998. A scholarly history of Israel during its first fifty years.

Haim Gordon, Rivca Gordon, and Taher Shriteh, *Beyond Intifada: Narratives of Freedom Fighters in the Gaza Strip*. Westport, CT: Praeger, 2003. An analysis of the first intifada, with first-person accounts from Palestinian "freedom fighters."

Baruch Kimmerling, *Politicide: Ariel Sharon's War Against the Palestinians*. New York: Verso, 2003. An indictment of Ariel Sharon, Israel's prime minister, and his efforts to destroy the political identity of the Palestinian people.

Reuters, *The Israeli-Palestinian Conflict: Crisis in the Middle East*. Upper Saddle River, NJ: Prentice-Hall PTR, 2003. This book provides a discussion of the second intifada along with personal stories from both Israelis and Palestinians and numerous annotated photographs depicting both sides of the conflict.

Andrew Rigby, *Living the Intifada*. London: Zed Books, 1991. This book looks at how everyday Palestinian life has been changed by the first intifada.

Eugene L. Rogan and Avi Shlaim, eds., *The War for Palestine*. New York: Cambridge University Press, 2001. A collection of essays discussing the 1948 War of Independence by Israeli, Arab, and Western historians and scholars.

Mark Tessler, *A History of the Israeli-Palestinian Conflict*. Bloomington: Indiana University Press, 1994. A comprehensive history of the Arab-Palestinian conflict from the origins of Zionism through the 1987 intifada.

Periodicals

Yasir Arafat, speech before the UN General Assembly on November 13, 1974, in "Palestine at the United Nations," *Journal of Palestine Studies*, vol. 4, no. 2, Winter 1975.

Associated Press, "Israeli Raid in Syria Alarms Arab World," *New York Times*, October 6, 2003.

————, "Sharon Defends Security Fence That Bush Has Criticized," *New York Times*, July 29, 2003.

Economist (U.S.), "After the War Is Over—Israel and Palestine," April 13, 2002.

————, "A Good Beginning: America, Israel and Palestine," June 7, 2003.

Thomas L. Friedman, "One Wall, One Man, One Vote," *New York Times*, September 15, 2003.

Efraim Karsh, "What Occupation?" *Commentary*, May 27, 2003.

Greg Myre, "Israel to Free Many Militants and Lift Some Roadblocks," *New York Times*, July 27, 2003.

New York Times, "Middle East Math," September 12, 2003.

Reuters, "Islamic Militant Groups Say Truce Dead After Israeli Strike," *New York Times*, August 21, 2003.

————, "Israeli Prisoner Release List Angers Palestinians," *New York Times*, August 4, 2003.

————, "Thousands Move to Jewish Settlements This Year," *New York Times*, July 24, 2003.

Internet Sources

BBC News, "Inside Arafat's Compound of Rubble," September 22, 2002. http://news.bbc.co.uk.

————, "Israel's History of Bomb Blasts," September 9, 2003. http://news.bbc.co.uk.

Bureau of Public Affairs, U.S. Department of State, "A Performance-Based Roadmap to a Permanent Two-State Solution to the Israeli-Palestinian Conflict," April 30, 2003. www.state.gov.

George W. Bush, remarks by the president on the Middle East, the White House, Washington, D.C., July 24, 2002. http://usinfo.state.gov.

————, speech at the American Enterprise Institute, Washington, D.C., February 26, 2003. http://usinfo.state.gov.

Christian Action for Israel, "The United Nations and Israel: General Assembly Resolution 194," 1996–2003. http://christianactionforisrael.org.

CNN International, "Arab States Back Road Map," June 3, 2003. http://edition.cnn.com.

Foundation for Middle East Peace, "Israeli Settlement in the Occupied Territories: A Guide," March 2002. www.fmep.org.

Haaretz Daily, "Israel's Road Map Reservations," www.haaretzdaily.com.

Conn Hallinan, "Road Map: Sharon and the Record," Foreign Policy

in Focus, June 20, 2003. www.fpif
.org.

Diego Ibarguen and Jonathan S. Landay,
"Arab Leaders Pledge to Crack Down
on Terror," Knight Ridder Newspapers,
June 3, 2003. www.realcities.com/mld/
krwashington/news/columnists/jonath
an_s_landay/600596 3.htm.

Israel Ministry of Foreign Affairs, "The
Balfour Declaration," www.mfa.gov.il/
mfa/go.asp?MFAH00pp0.

————, "Statement by Prime Minister
Barak on His Return from the Camp
David Summit," www.mfa.gov.il/mfa/
go.asp?MFAH0hnu0.

————, "The Wye River Memorandum,"
www.mfa.gov.il/mfa/go.asp?MFAH07
or0.

Jewish Virtual Library, "The Irgun," www
.us-israel.org.

————, "Mahmoud Abbas." www.us
-israel.org.

Kate Milner, "Who Are the Suicide
Bombers?" BBC News, December 2,
2001. http://news.bbc.co.uk.

Palestine Facts, "What Took Place at
Camp David in 2000?" www.palestine
facts.org.

K. Subrahmanyam, "Go Back to Oslo:
Land for Palestine, Peace for Israel,"
Times of India, September 15, 2003.
http://meadev.nic.in.

U.S. News Service, "Statement of the
Task Force on Palestinian Reform,"
February 20, 2003. www.reliefweb
.int/w/rwb.nsf/0/db8c82761e1944b5
85256cd3005c5c73?OpenDocument.

Kelly Wallace, "Sharon: 'Occupation'
Terrible for Israel, Palestinians," CNN
International, May 27, 2003. www
.cnn.com/2003/WORLD/meast/057/
26/mideast.

World Bank, "Two Years of *Intifada*,
Closures, and the Palestinian Economic Crisis," March 5, 2003. http://
worldbank.org.

Yale Law School, the Avalon Project,
"British White Paper of 1939," www
.yale.edu.

INDEX

Egypt
  Camp David Accords
    and, 42
  peace efforts by, 39
  Six-Day War and,
    31–32
  Suez-Sinai War and,
    28–30
  treatment of Palestinians
    by, 59
  War of Attrition and,
    33
  War of Independence
    and, 26, 27
  Yom Kippur War and,
    36, 38
elections
  Israeli (1992), 58–59
  Palestinian (1996), 61
Entebbe raid, 43
Europe
  Jewish emigration from,
    14
  Zionist movement in,
    14–15
European Union, 77
Exodus (ship), 25

al-Fatah, 33, 34
fedayeen, 28
Fez Plan, 49
Fighters for Freedom, 22
First Zionist Congress,
  15
France, 17, 29

Galilee, Sea of, 31
Gaza, 42
Gemayel, Bashir, 48
Germany, 20–21
Golan Heights, 32
Great Britain
  Arab rebellion against,
    21

attack on Egypt sup-
  ported by, 29
conflicting promises by,
  15–17
inquiry into Arab-Israeli
  violence by, 18–19
Jewish immigration and,
  19, 20, 22
King-Crane Commission
  and, 17
rule in Palestine by,
  17–18
Jewish resistance
  against, 22, 23
Suez Canal and, 29
Gulf War (1990), 56–58

Haganah, the, 22, 25
Hamas, 56, 60, 70–71,
  83
Haniyah, Ismail al-, 83
Hebron, 42, 66, 83
Herzl, Theodor, 15
Hizballah, 62
Husayn ibn 'Ali, 16
Hussein, Saddam, 56–58
Hussein I (king of Jordan)
  on Jordanian-Israeli
    relations, 62
  peace efforts by, 49–50
  PLO and, 34

International Monetary
  Fund, 79
International Red Cross,
  74
intifada, 12–13
  1987, 50–53
  2000, 69–70
    economic impact of, 78
    high cost of, 74, 76
    Israeli violence following,
      72–74
Iraq, 26, 56–58

Irgun Zvai Leumi, 22, 23
Islamic Jihad, 62, 70–71
Israel
  birth of, 23, 24–25
  Camp David Accords
    and, 41–42
  economic attacks on
    economy of, 52–53
  house arrest of Arafat
    by, 75
  lands seized by, 10
  Lebanon invaded by,
    43–45, 47–48
  Madrid Peace Conference
    and, 58
  Palestinian politics and,
    43
  peace movement in, 46
  peace proposal/efforts
    by, 56, 62
  PLO recognition of, 55,
    56
  politics of, 39
  removal of settlements
    and, 88
  resistance against British
    rule by, 22, 23
  response to intifadas by,
    51–52, 53, 72–73
  on Road Map peace
    plan, 81
  security for, 64, 83–85
  Six-Day War and,
    31–32
  Suez-Sinai War and,
    28–30
  violence by, 13, 45, 47,
    83
  War of Independence
    and, 26–27
  Yom Kippur War and, 37
  see also Jewish settle-
    ments
Israeli Knesset, 40, 41

Boone County Public Library

Customer ID: 204017820602
Circulation system messages:
Patron status is ok.

Title: The Arab-Israeli conflict
ID: 204091004248293
Due: 2/9/2008 11:59 PM
Circulation system messages:
Item checkout ok.

Total items: 1
1/19/2008 8:35 AM

Thank you for using BCPL.
www.bcpl.org
859.342.BOOK

PICTURE CREDITS

Cover image: Getty Images
Alaa Badarneh/EPA/Landov, 12
AP/Wide World Photos, 46, 51, 55, 63, 65
© Bettmann/CORBIS, 35
© Bernard Bisson/CORBIS, 49
DPA/Landov, 89
Getty Images, 48, 72
Abed al-Hafiz Hashlamoun/EPA/Landov, 78
Nayef Hashlamoun/Reuters/Landov, 87

© Hulton/Archive by Getty Images, 15, 19, 23, 27, 30, 37, 41, 60
Ali Jarekji/Reuters/Landov, 47
Gil Cohen Magen/Reuters/Landov, 75
William Philpott/Reuters/Landov, 76
© Patrick Robert/CORBIS SYGMA, 52
© David Rubinger/CORBIS, 44, 45, 57
© Pablo San Juan/CORBIS, 64
Mohammed Saber/EPA/Landov, 82
Rusty Stewart/EPA/Landov, 70
Mafouz Abu Turk/Reuters/Landov, 85

ABOUT THE AUTHOR

Debra A. Miller is a writer and lawyer with an interest in current events and history. She began her law career in Washington, D.C., where she worked on legislative, policy, and legal matters in government, public interest, and private law firm positions. She now lives with her husband in Encinitas, California. Miller has written and edited numerous publications for legal publishers, as well as books and anthologies on historical and political topics.